Roger Hutchinson is an author and journalist. In 1977 he joined the *West Highland Free Press*, for which newspaper he is still a columnist. His book *The Soap Man: Lewis, Harris and Lord Leverhulme* was shortlisted for the Saltire Scottish Book of the Year in 2004 and his bestselling *Calum's Road* was shortlisted for the Royal Society of Literature's Ondaatje Prize in 2007.

Praise for *Polly: The True Story behind 'Whisky Galore'*

'Fascinating'
Sunday Post

'A sparkling crystal glass of a book . . .
Heroic, hilarious and heartwarming'
The Herald

'Riveting . . . a legendary tale, full of humour'
West Highland Free Press

'In this impressive and authoritative book, Roger Hutchinson reveals the reality behind the romance and comes as near to the truth as is possible'
Derek Cooper

POLLY

The True Story Behind 'Whisky Galore'

ROGER HUTCHINSON

BIRLINN

This edition first published in 2024 by
Birlinn Limited
West Newington House
10 Newington Road
Edinburgh
EH9 1QS

www.birlinn.co.uk

First published in 1990 by Mainstream Publishing Company (Edinburgh) Ltd

ISBN 978 1 78027 850 6

British Library Cataloguing-in-Publication Data
A catalogue record of this book is available on request from the British Library

Typeset by HewerText (UK) Ltd, Edinburgh

Papers used by Birlinn are from well-managed forests and other responsible sources

Printed and bound by Clays Ltd, Elcograf S.p.A.

To William Hutchinson, who fought in the Sea War

Contents

Introduction   ix

1 The Backdrop   1
2 Islands at War   3
3 Sleek and Handsome Vessels   26
4 The King's Ransom   46
5 Men at Work   60
6 Not Guilty   79
7 To the Bottom of the Sea   106
8 The Fillums   127

Postscript   149
Bibliography   151
Index   153

Introduction

'It was the best year of my life.
We had so much fun out of her'
– Eriskay woman

I first crossed the Sound of Eriskay in the late 1970s. That was closer in time to 1941, the year of the SS *Politician*, than I am now to 1979. Much has changed in the Outer Hebrides since the crossings of 40 years ago. There was then no causeway between South Uist and Eriskay – it was not slung across the white sand seabed until the beginning of the 21st century – although its presence would not have astonished people: Uist was no stranger to causeways.

There were also no car ferries operating in the vicinity. Eriskay and Uist and Barra were connected by small passenger craft operated by independent local men. The nationalised services run by Caledonian MacBrayne only plied the longer deep-sea routes to and from mainland ports. So when, on a still and sunny Sunday afternoon in 1980, I travelled over the neighbouring Sound of Barra with a football team from South Uist – they to play a league fixture, me to spectate – it was aboard a clinker-built open boat with an inboard engine and a crew of one.

There is a gay abundance of stories, true and apocryphal, of the escapades which surrounded the affair of the *Politician*. I have reluctantly omitted, or at best only alluded to, those which have not been confirmed by at least one primary source. Fortunately, not many slipped through that net, but it does mean that I have left out of the main text a story I was told by a Uist footballer that day in 1980 which helped to persuade me of the possibility of writing this book.

The tale in question involved the footballer's father and uncle. In the summer of 1941, they were keeping several boxes of *Polly* whisky company on a sailing smack which, when suddenly alarmed and pursued by a fast and vengeful motorised excise launch, took shelter behind an islet in the Sound of Barra. Before the excise launch came into view, they lowered their sail and mast and scuttled their own boat with its cargo in the high tide, hiding themselves in the long grass of the islet, and consequently disappearing like a sorcerer's trick from the surface of the sea. Six hours later, when the tide turned and the bemused excise launch had gone, they refloated their boat and its cargo on the incoming water and set sail for home.

I particularly regret this story's absence from the book, partly because it was the first original story recounted to me about the *Polly*, and partly because it was told by people from the islands who still communicated enormous pleasure in that lively and mischievous time out of war which was taken by their forebears in the otherwise gloomy months of 1941.

I do not regret giving as wide a berth as possible to apochrypha. Inevitably, in the peat fire glow of west Highland history, fantasy jostles with fact for living space, and fantasy often wins.

In 1990, when I was writing *Polly*, there were widespread rumours about the function of the Jamaican currency notes which were loaded on the ship at Liverpool. Their actual purpose was mundane. Like much of the rest of the world, and almost all of the British world, Jamaica's banknotes were then prepared and printed by the established specialist company De La Rue of London. During the Second World War, Jamaica required ten-shilling, one-pound and five-pound notes as much as she had in peacetime. They were not a priority, however, so eight caseloads of them were loaded onto an unescorted cargo vessel which was then instructed to call into the Caribbean on its way to New Orleans with a quarter of a million bottles of best Scotch whisky. Most of them got no further than the Sound of Eriskay.

As news of the banknotes leaked out, before and after the first publication of this book, conspiracy theories blossomed. They were, broadly speaking, inspired by nothing but a desire for conspiracy theories. The most seductive, which has filled several newspaper feature pages in recent years, involve the payment of some sort of bribe or sweetener to the troublesome Duke and Duchess of Windsor, who had in 1940 been offloaded from Europe to the governor's mansion in the Bahamas.

It has never been satisfactorily explained why the British Government needed to give Wallis Simpson and the former King Edward VIII £3 million pounds in Jamaican ten-bob notes when there were perfectly discreet banks, which dealt in less obvious quantities of more suitable currencies, in Nassau and the United States. The answer is that the British Government did not need to do any such thing. In the absence of satisfactory explanations, let alone evidence, this theory is best left to gather dust.

In his characteristically generous Introduction to an earlier edition of this book, the late Derek Cooper wrote that the story of the SS *Politician*, "so elaborately handwoven in the Western Isles", could not have "reached such legendary proportions anywhere else. If the ship had run aground off Dover or Hull it would have been towed away and forgotten within a week. But the *Polly*, a remarkable gift from God, lubricated the imagination of the islanders. It has become in the last half century an enduring myth."

Derek was of course right. In fiction and non-fiction, this story represents a perfect blend of subject-matter and place. In his creation of *Whisky Galore*, Compton Mackenzie had to imagine very little. There was nonetheless an understory, a counterblast to the mythical narrative. It reminds us that even in the Scottish Hebrides, 1941 was a perilous, paranoid moment in the Second World War, and that legends are usually bright tapestries woven around grittier, darker, actual events. It also reminds us that the best examples of wit and hilarity are found as often in the real world as in the better comic novels.

As well as the people who are named in the book, I would like to thank Brian Montague, Allan McDonald, Cailean Maclean, Dr Alasdair Maclean, Graeme Cubbin, archivist at Thos. & Jas. Harrison Ltd, Liverpool, and Jim Jump of the National Union of Seamen. Without the libraries and filing systems of Sabhal Mor Ostaig, the Clan Donald Centre, the National Records Offices in Edinburgh and in London, the General Register and Record of Shipping and Seamen in Cardiff, South Uist Estates, the Customs & Excise, and the British Film Institute, this book could not have been researched.

In its first 34 years *Polly* has now been published by three different companies. It's time to settle down, and I'm particularly grateful for this latest Birlinn edition to Hugh Andrew, Mark Stanton, Andrew Simmons and Abigail Salvesen. They know why.

Roger Hutchinson
Isle of Raasay
January 2024

MAPS

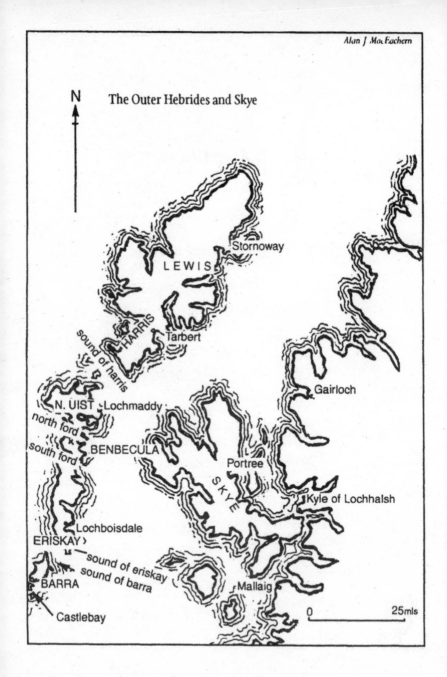

Alan J MacEachern

N

The Outer Hebrides and Skye

Stornoway

LEWIS

sound of harris

HARRIS

Tarbert

Gairloch

N. UIST · Lochmaddy

north ford

south ford

BENBECULA

Portree

SKYE

Kyle of Lochhalsh

Lochboisdale

ERISKAY

sound of eriskay

sound of barra

BARRA

Mallaig

Castlebay

0   25mls

Alan J Maceachern

The Sound of Eriskay

ONE

The Backdrop

Cha dànaig gaoth riamh nach robh an seòl feareigin.
A wind never blew that did not fill somebody's sail.
— Hebridean saying

Shortly after daybreak on the damp, overcast morning of 5 February 1941, a teenaged boy left his home in the secluded South Uist village of South Glendale to walk, barefooted, eastward along the empty shore. A mile away to his right, plainly visible even in such mournful weather, stood the scattered stone cottages of Bunmhullin and Rosinish at the north end of the island of Eriskay. To his left the rock-strewn, brown heather hills of the Uists rolled quietly up into the mist. Between them lay a narrow sea-sound, scored and broken by numerous reefs and so shallow that the vaguest ray of sunlight turned its clear water into a startling shade of Arctic blue and glistened on its bed of pure white sand.

A strong wind had blown throughout the previous night and the boy was beachcombing. It was a routine expedition, which over the last 17 months of war had brought rewards uncommon to peacetime. Occasionally the youth had been obliged to spend several hours harvesting on the rocks and the gravel and the sandy coves, but on that morning his walk was quickly ended. Within a few minutes he had doubled back and was racing into the village. Banging on the unlocked doors of houses a croft's width apart, he began to shout: "*Bata mor air an sgeir! Tha bata mor air an sgeir!*" ("Ship aground! There's a big ship aground!")

TWO

Islands at War

Nuair thig bàillidh ùr bidh lagh ùr 'na chois.
When a new factor comes he brings a new law with him.
– Hebridean saying

The southern islands of the Outer Hebrides archipelago are a file of gentle mounds sitting gracefully in 60 miles of sea between latitudes 56.57 N and 57.65 N. As the crow flies they are never less than 50 miles from the mainland of north-west Scotland, and two hours by ferry from the nearest of the islands of the Inner Hebrides. Across the Atlantic and on the eastern continental landmass such northerly points are haunted by icebergs and held in permafrost, but the Hebridean seaboard of Great Britain is kept, if not warm, at least habitable by the happy accident of the Gulf Stream, which brushes its promontories and its stretches of deserted sand with the remnants of warm Caribbean seas before finally foundering, spent and cold, in the waters of Scandinavia.

These are not particularly mountainous islands. From North Uist and Benbecula, down through South Uist, Eriskay, Barra, Vatersay and the string of depopulated islets which drift for 20 miles south of there like so many discarded lizards' tails, there is not a hill which stands higher than 2,000 feet. The deranged volcanic peaks of Skye and of the Moidart and Arisaig mainland

Polly

are almost always to be seen from the southern isles; while they themselves, when they are visible from the east, look to be no more than the domes of the heads of a distant crowd, shuffling modestly over the horizon.

The people who live between the rolling Atlantic *machair* and the granite coves which face the Minch, between adventurous fishing and subsistence agriculture, are the repository of one of the oldest cultures in Europe. They were among the first in Scotland to receive Christianity in place of druidism, to blend the Irish Gaelic language and culture with Pictish ritual and ceremony, and to this day they embrace both their Catholic faith and their ancient tongue with vigour and affection. These are idiosyncratic traits in the 20th century and they are, of course, partly the results of geographical isolation. A necessary autonomy of mind and spirit has been forged here, among wind and rock and sea, on islands which for the greatest part of their history have lived independent of the outside world. In some respects they are independent even of their Hebridean neighbours. Thanks largely to the apostolic efforts of three 17th-century Irish priests, Fathers Hegarty, Ward and Duggan, the people of the islands south of the North Ford which separates Benbecula from North Uist were reconciled to Catholicism rather than to Protestantism at that time of seismic religious upheaval, and they have remained among the most loyal adherents to the Church of Rome in Britain – sharing a culture, a local government and a ferry service with some of the staunchest Presbyterians. Had Father Dermit Duggan, his instruction to and baptism of the islands up to and including Benbecula completed, not contracted an illness and died in 1657, while he was planning his first missionary visit to North Uist, the theological history of the Hebrides may have been quite different. As it is, the dividing line between the two faiths – a line invisible to most outsiders – lies still where Father Duggan's dreams fell, between Benbecula and North Uist.

But independence has not, in the southern isles at least, meant solitude. The Gaels of the Hebrides have always been seamen of outstanding quality. They have travelled the known world as free and willing sailors, in missionary curraghs, crusading galleys, medieval barques of trade and war, whaling and fishing fleets, cutters of the Empire, battleships, cruisers and destroyers of the Royal Navy and steamers of the merchant marines. Their seamanship, especially in small boats under sail, became legendary in the 19th and early 20th centuries; and the extent of their travels was awesome. You are more likely, a visitor would be told, to find a man from Barra or from South Uist who can draw you street maps of Shanghai and San Francisco, than one who has visited Lochmaddy. Writing of the seamen of his native island in 1941, the Barra doctor Donald Buchanan remembered how, "On boarding a Blue Funnel liner once, on the quarantine anchorage at Singapore, I found that six members of the crew were my neighbours in Barra: some of them still remind me of the meeting. A few weeks later I was spending a holiday on the cruising liner *Warilda* in Northern Queensland, when one of the first members of the crew I noticed was Roderick McDougall from Kentangval. Very shortly afterwards, while on board one of Burns Phillips' mail-boats at Port Moresby in remote New Guinea, the first man to confront me was Jonathan McNeil, of Glen Castlebay . . ." Island doctors, it must be observed, also did their share of globe-trotting.

Hebrideans entertained their own motley band of visitors, before and since the apostolic Irish. The shoguns of Scandinavia held a tenuous sovereignty here until 1266, and the Norsemen left their blood, their place-names and family-names on the rocky shores of the east and the fertile grasslands of the west.

The people of the islands have since received, with variable humour, the ambassadors of foreign religions, educationalists using an unwelcome language and representatives of the authority of distant governments. They have become accustomed to outside interference in their lives and have grown to tolerate it.

In 1941 that tolerance was severely strained. Given the perverse, chaotic events in the southern isles in the 101 years which preceded the outbreak of the Second World War in September 1939, it is a wonder that it did not snap.

In 1838 the islands from Benbecula to Barra Head were united under a brand new overlord. For centuries since the early Middle Ages, throughout the lamented Lordship of the Isles and into and after the Jacobite uprisings of the 18th century, the southern isles had been owned, if not entirely governed, by their hereditary clan chiefs. Barra and its southern satellites had been the fiefdom of the MacNeils by charter since 1427, and in Benbecula, South Uist and Eriskay the Clanranald sept of Clan Donald had held sway since the retreat of the Vikings. Two decades of vain folly finally put an end to centuries of familial continuity. In Barra in the 1830s Lieutenant-General Roderick MacNeil took to the unsoldierly world of business. In an attempt to maximise his profits from the kelp industry (the seaweed which was being gathered in great quantity from the shores of the islands) he built a large processing factory at Northbay. It failed and his creditors foreclosed and sequestrated the estate.

And in Uist, Ranald George MacDonald of Clanranald had long since decided, in common with many of his peers, that the life of a Regency buck was infinitely better fun than that of a Highland chieftain, and proceeded to throw good money after bad in the society life of Gothenburg and Park Lane. He had, to be fair, come of age with debts of £47,000 inherited from his

father, John of Moidart, the 19th of Clanranald, but Ranald
George did nothing to restore the family fortune, and by 1838
he, too, was obliged to sell his islands.

The lands of Clanranald and MacNeil found one buyer, a
successful Aberdeenshire landowner, Lieutenant-Colonel John
Gordon of Cluny Castle. Gordon was, in the jargon of his
time, an "improver", which is to say that he had no patience
with "unprofitable" estates and that he recognised no claim to
the land other than the bottom line of his accountant's audit.
In the southern isles he found, as MacNeil and Clanranald
could have told him, tracts of land which were hugely unprofitable to their nominal owner and which were occupied by a
race of people who showed an obdurate fondness for living
there. Having laid out almost £120,000 for these distant parts,
Gordon had a problem. Unlike lush Aberdeenshire estates the
Hebrides were not tailored to make any profit at all from spec-
ulative landowners. It was as much as their native people could
do, using the careful, thrifty agricultural and fishing practices
of their forebears, to support themselves, let alone the unrequested ambitions of Lieutenant-Colonel John Gordon and
his retinue. These were pre-crofting communities, townships
which shared not only the same common grazings, but the
same unfenced fields of barley, oats, rye and potatoes, and in
doing so required the use of virtually all the islands' arable
land. It did not take John Gordon long to be convinced that
the major obstacle to his "improvement" of the Uists and Barra
was the indigenous population.

So he set about removing them. The clearances of the southern isles in the middle of the last century did not become
a *cause célèbre* at the time, as did many on the mainland;
the name of John Gordon was never as vilified as those of the
Duke of Sutherland, Patrick Sellar and James Loch. But in the

1840s and the 1850s Lieutenant-Colonel John Gordon, anxious to establish a chain of sheep farms from Nunton in Benbecula to Vatersay, south of Barra, showed a wonderful appetite for eviction and forced emigration. All the familiar tableaux of the clearances were acted out in the southern isles: old women were harassed from their homes under threat of having the roof removed, young men were hunted down on their township lands and forced, struggling and shouting, to the piers at Lochboisdale and Castlebay and on to hulks such as the notorious *Admiral,* bound for Quebec and the uncharted wastes of Upper Canada. When it met 30 years later, the Napier Commission, set up by the Government to investigate the problems of the crofting areas, was told by one old man that 1,700 people "from the North Ford to Barra Head" had been transported in the early years of Colonel Gordon's "improvements".

His estimation was a modest one. The emigrants arrived in Canada without money, work or food. A letter in the *Quebec Times* in 1851 execrated the "savage cruelty" of Colonel Gordon and "the atrocity of the deed". Seventy concerned Canadians put their signatures to this letter, which pointed out:

> The 1,500 souls whom Colonel Gordon has sent to Quebec this season have all been supported for the past week at least, and conveyed to Upper Canada at the expense of the colony, and on their arrival in Toronto and Hamilton, the greater number have been dependent on the charity of the benevo-lent for a morsel of bread. Four hundred are in the river at present and will arrive in a day or two, *making a total of nearly 2,000* of Colonel Gordon's tenants and cottars whom the province will have to support. The winter is at hand . . . where are these people to find food?

In 1841 the combined population of Benbecula, South Uist and Eriskay was 7,333. By 1861 it was down to 5,358. During the same period the population of Barra and its southerly outposts – most of which were, at the time, inhabited – fell from 2,363 to 1,853. Some of these people may have gone to Nairn and the Moray Firth, and to Glasgow during the famine caused by the potato rot of the early 1840s, but they were a minority. Most of them sailed on the *Admiral* and her sisters, pausing only briefly at Stornoway to be joined by a contingent of Sir William Matheson's evictees from Lewis before bidding goodbye to the islands for ever. Most of them, in fact, were removed by the factors and the ground officers of Lieutenant-Colonel John Gordon, supported by the full majesty of the law.

For the law was not only powerless to halt Gordon's outrages, it was positively on his side. The law said that the land was his to "improve". The law gave him the freedom and authority to set impossible rents and to evict when those rents were not paid. The law had no brief for an island community largely ignorant of the English language and entirely innocent of the caprices of the British legal system. To the people of the southern isles, the law was no friend.

Of the majority that remained in the islands, many entire families, even whole townships, found themselves moved from the fertile *machair* land up to the rough, heather-blanketed heath in the foothills of the eastern mountains, land which they had previously used only for shielings and summer grazings. But most found themselves to be increasingly dependent on the sea, for the munificent sea was always there, unfenced and free from enclosure. Some of its fruits, such as kelp and herring, were responsible for times of comparative affluence; its driftwood furnished houses; in times of hardship its more modest offerings, such as common shellfish, sustained life. The faithfully

Catholic people of the southern isles named many of their natural treasures after the Virgin, and all of the produce of the sea
was embraced in one term: *cuile Mhoire,* the treasure chest of
Mary. Without the sea these people could not have defied the
efforts of Lieutenant-Colonel John Gordon.

Gordon shortly found that even sheep-farming was a hazardous investment in the Uists and Barra, but before he died he
made one final effort to settle his southern isles problem. He
made a proposal to the Government which was, even for the
time, so breathtakingly deranged that we would be inclined to
doubt it now, if it had not been dutifully recorded by a member
of the Napier Commission, Mr Charles Fraser Macintosh.
Mindful of the great expense incurred in transporting convicts
across the world to Australia, Gordon suggested to the
Government of Queen Victoria that the islands of South Uist
and Benbecula, if cleared of their native population, would serve
equally well as a penal colony. Gordon was, wrote Fraser
Macintosh later, "ready to dispose of it as such to Government,
no doubt first clearing off the whole population". The
Government, after due consideration, declined the Colonel's
offer.

In 1878 the islands were inherited by Gordon's daughter-in-
law, Lady Gordon Cathcart. She found a people who were no
longer prepared to be silent about their grievances. This was a
time of land hunger throughout the Highlands and nowhere
were the pangs more acute than on the scattered islands which
formed the more distant reaches of Lady Cathcart's new estate.
Articulate, radical spokesmen had come forth in every district.
There was Michael Buchanan in Barra, who waited outside the
church of Our Lady Star of the Sea in Castlebay every Sunday to
follow the priest with "Michael's sermon". There was Father
Donald McColl, the parish priest to the north end of South

Uist. And there was Angus MacPhee, who had been born in Torlum, Benbecula, in the early years of the century and had lived through all of the "dislocations"; in his seventies he found himself on heather land where "it has become impossible for us to live". These men testified to the Napier Commission when, in 1883, it arrived in the southern isles to inquire into the condition of the crofting communities. The Napier Commission's reports resulted in the Crofting Act of 1886, which gave crofters security of tenure, but the Crofting Act did too little for the people of the Uists and Barra, for in order to enjoy security of tenure, a family had first to have a croft.

The congestion of landless families in the islands, which was brought about not only by the establishment of sheep farms, but also by the quite gratuitous clearing of such smaller islands as Mingulay, coincided with a decline in the treasury of *cuile Mhoire*. The kelp industry, whose profits had always been assiduously raked away by the estate but which, at its peak, had paid a quantity of exchangeable currency in return for hours of backbreaking work (as much as one pound a day for a whole family, working morning to night, at the end of the 19th century) was in decline. And the west coast herring fishing was under siege.

It is salutary to reflect now that as late as the last century the west coast fishermen of the islands and the deep inshore lochs were the aristocrats of the Scottish fishing industry. Using longlines, made from imported hemp and deposited overnight on Atlantic banks, theirs was a conservative industry. The lines brought home only select numbers of the choicest fish. For quality, they were unbeatable. For indiscriminate quantity, they were driven from the water by the trawling nets of the east coast adventurers who were, by the turn of the 20th century, already arriving in numbers to exploit the waters of the west. The southern isles were not, at this time, a happy place. Ada Goodrich-Freer, an inquisitive and sympathetic visitor to the islands in 1900, wrote two years later that South Uist was

> . . . as separate from all that is human, kindly, genial, as if it were a suburb of the North Pole. There is, thank Heaven, but one South Uist in the world, though in poverty, misery, and neglect, the island of Barra, sixteen miles south, runs it very close . . . South Uist is surely the most forsaken spot on God's earth.

In spite of some concessions of land, wrenched, on behalf of the people, by the tardy action of the Crofters' Commission, the greater part of the island is under sheep farms, a "farm" here signifying a tract of country once bright with happy homesteads, now laid bare and desolate. Heaps of grey stone scattered all over the island are all that remain of once thriving cottages; narrow strips of greener grass or more tender heather are all that is left to represent waving cornfields and plots of fertile ground handed on from generation to generation of home-loving agriculturalists. The more hardy and vigorous of the race which once flour- ished here are now scattered over the face of the earth; the old, the weak, the spiritless, for the most part, have alone remained, and their children, white-faced, anaemic, depressed, driven to the edge of the sea as one after another the scraps of land redeemed by their perilous industry were taken from them, are still fighting hand-to-hand with Nature, almost worn out with a hopeless struggle. They are the only Highlanders I ever met who were curt in manner, almost inhospitable, discourteous; but one soon learns to forgive what, after all, is but the result of long years of life "on the defensive" . . . The very existence of the island of

South Uist is itself a tragedy which shames our civilisation.
Nowhere in our proud Empire is there a spot more desolate,
grim, hopelessly poverty-stricken.

Sixty-one years of the Gordon family had indeed bred in the
naturally courteous people of the southern isles a fierce mistrust
of interfering outsiders – a mistrust which could at times erupt
into outright hostility. The outraged Mrs Goodrich-Freer may
have been in the islands at the same time as a "sportsman" named
C.V.A. Peel, who wrote from London in 1901:

Much of the pleasure of shooting in the Outer Hebrides is
spoilt by the conduct of the crofters. It is not conducive to
sport to be followed by a gang of men and ordered out of the
country, nor is it pleasant to be cursed in Gaelic by a crowd
of irate old women, even if you do not understand every
word they say. They accused us of shooting their horses and
sheep, filled in the pits which we had dug in the sandhills for
geese, shouted to put up geese we were stalking, cut up the
canvas and broke the seats of our folding boat, and tried in
every way possible to spoil our sport. They were especially
insolent and troublesome in Benbecula and Barra. Taking
them as a whole, the crofters are an ignorant lot of creatures,
and the less said about them the better.

Indignation was turning into militancy in the southern isles,
and once it had identified its target it would not be denied.

The first land raids took place on Barra in the closing years of
the 19th century. A group of men led by William Og MacNeil
of the overcrowded village of Bruernish at the east of the island
coveted and began to stake claims to the green pasturelands of
Eoligarry. After a number of "incidents" the Local Government

Board intervened, bought Eoligarry from the Gordon Estate and settled a number of crofters there.

But the prime target for the landless men of Barra was the grassy sward of Vatersay, a substantial island directly to the south of Castlebay which was used, in its entirety, by the Gordon Estate as a sheep farm. The remaining population of Mingulay and the people who found an occasional income from Lady Cathcart's proud new fishing station in Castlebay insufficient, set their sights on Vatersay. In 1906 they seized the island, rowing across to erect huts and put their cattle out to pasture. The Gordon Estate had the local sheriff serve an interdict, but it was simply ignored, and in 1909 the Local Government Board, after three years of cautious debate and circuitous cold war, stepped forward to buy Vatersay for £6,250 as a crofting estate. The old farm building remained the property of Lady Cathcart: it was not to be touched, and although its owner and her representatives never again set foot inside it, the great house stands still today, a gaunt, roofless ruin above the quiet settlement of Vatersay.

A curiously wilful gesture marred the reclaiming of Vatersay. The Government refused to grant a tenancy there to the most active and open of the land raiders and when they refused to move from their squatted lands writs were issued and, this time, acted upon. Not for the last time in the southern isles, men went to prison for claiming what they believed to be rightfully theirs.

The land seizures spread through the other islands like a muirburn. A Land Act of 1911 gave the Land Court the power to appraise compulsory compensation to landowners unwilling to release their farms into crofting, and when men returning to the "land fit for heroes" from the First World War received the information that in the defeated nation, Germany, an estimated 93 per cent of agricultural land was owned by smallholders,

agitation reached a new height. In August 1919 the Land
Settlement Measure gave the Board of Agriculture, Scotland,
enlarged powers of compulsory purchase, and a bonus of
£2,750,000 to spend. The BOAS was not left idle. Over the
following 15 years farm after farm on the Gordon Estate was
raided, seized and settled. The central authorities in Edinburgh
and London, particularly under the National Government of
Ramsay Macdonald from 1922 to 1924, became increasingly
reluctant to act on behalf of Highland landowners against their
crofters. Lady Gordon Cathcart received, at her Bournemouth
home in 1923 and 1924, letters of frustration and despair from
her factor in South Uist, John MacDonald. The raiders, he told
his employer,

> . . . are now under the impression that they are all right and
> that they will have the support of the House of Commons . . .
> I suppose there is no help for it and one must submit . . . in
> view of the smashing up of all the other farms on your lady-
> ship's property there does not seem to be any gain in retaining
> Nunton or Nunton Hill farms . . . there would seem to be a
> spirit of defiance throughout both islands [Benbecula and
> South Uist] amongst the young men.

Claims of land starvation and hardship issuing from the
southern isles were, factor MacDonald assured Lady Cathcart,

> . . . all "humbug" and appear to have been engineered by one
> or two rank Socialists who, to gain popularity, started the ball
> rolling. Throughout South Uist, Benbecula and Barra there is
> no such thing as destitution. That there is some poverty is
> undoubted but then it is not more acute today than it has
> always been . . .

John MacDonald's "rank Socialists" did a thorough job. Throughout the 1920s he could hardly turn around without seeing another stretch of grazing or arable land being seized and grazed with crofters' cattle and horses, or put under the plough for winter feed. By the end of that decade the spirit of the sheep farm had been exorcised from the southern isles. And by the time of the death of Lady Gordon Cathcart in 1932, when the whole estate was left in the hands of Trustees, the wildly unstable plans of her family for Benbecula, South Uist, Eriskay and Barra, their designs for penal colonies, fishing stations, forced emigrations and vainglorious resettlement schemes, seemed no more than the shadow of a passing cloud. The land of the southern isles was, more or less, in the hands of its people.

Those people made the most of their few years of peace and stability. The 1930s were depressed years in Britain, but new tiled, stone-built, two-storey houses were built to replace many of the small thatched cottages which had scattered picturesquely across the landscape of Uist and Barra. The small, sturdy, multi-functional island horses which had monopolised much of the winter feed were supplemented by the introduction of an occasional tractor to the *machairs* of the west coast – land which is still the best worked in the crofting counties and a monument to the people who won it back from sheep farming. The kelp industry survived, encouraged by the growing demand for iodine (which, among a startling array of other products, could be processed from the weed), but on a more civilised basis, with crofters supplying directly to local factories. The herring fishing continued its inexorable decline. As the sophisticated markets of the old and the new worlds came to reject salted, barrelled fish in favour of produce from tins, so the days passed when it was possible to walk across Castle Bay on the decks of trawlers. The

Barra catch in 1914 was counted as the lowest ever, at a value of £27,343 landed by 990 fishermen on 310 sailing boats. But by 1939 the Labour MP for the Western Isles, Malcolm K. MacMillan, was reporting to the House of Commons that his constituency's fishing industry "is almost in ruins today". Some men turned to creel fishing for lobster and other "fancy fish", others supplemented their summer income with seasonal work in the shipyards of the Clyde or in the Glasgow Corporation's gas plant. Young women who had once gutted herring, filleting up to 100,000 fish a day in a mesmeric whirl of wrist action and thin blade, now sought employment as domestics in the bourgeois houses of the south.

But the 20th century made slow progress towards the southern isles. At the outbreak of the Second World War there was no electricity in the islands other than that which was supplied by the private generators attached to the hotels and to the houses of a few professional men. There was no piped water. Steamships such as the *Dunara Castle* and the *Lochearn* arrived from the mainland, seas permitting, at Lochboisdale and Castlebay every other day. An air service had started in 1937 between Renfrew and the Traigh Mhor in Barra, the wide, white cockle strand upon which an aeroplane can land only at low tide, an idiosyncrasy which has gifted opening paragraphs to travel writers for five decades.

There were, in 1939, no causeways connecting South Uist to Benbecula and Benbecula to North Uist; their only approaches were across two hazardous stretches of tidal strand. There were few lorries and fewer cars but, particularly in Uist, a host of sturdy sit-up-and-beg bicycles bought in by mail order from A. Smart of London. On Sundays the road for a quarter of a mile to either side of St Peter's Church, Daliburgh, was practically bordered with Mr Smart's parked products.

In 1939 Barra was finally ringed by a tarmacadamed road. This was largely the result of a truculent, relentless campaign which had been conducted by a well-connected elderly writer named Compton Mackenzie, who had settled six years earlier at the western end of the Traigh Mhor, overlooking Eriskay and the hills of South Uist and the islets, reefs and sand-beds of the sea-sounds of the southern isles.

Throughout the 1930s the southern isles had been a rich recruiting ground for the Territorial Army. Units were established in North and South Uist, as well as in Skye and, in the early months of 1939, in Harris. In those depressed years the annual camp provided a subsidised trip away from the croft in the company of friends, to places on the mainland of Scotland and England. "It was the best way for getting a fortnight's holiday away from the island and enjoying yourselves," one man recalled later. "I don't think it was patriotism. For some it might have been, but not as far as I was concerned. The other boys went and you all went for a fortnight to camp and had a good time." Teenagers from throughout the islands signed up at Drill Halls, such as those at Liniclate and Carnan, most of them never expecting war, and not one of them expecting that when war came they and their fellow crofters and fishermen who were called up to form the backbone of the 51st Highland Division would suffer a swift, cruel and ignominious defeat.

The Territorials were mobilised the moment war was declared. Plans to extend the Drill Halls in Uist were promptly scrapped; there was to be no more playing at soldiers in the Highlands and Islands. The Territorials, now Cameron Highlanders, gathered in Aldershot where, by the spring of 1940, they were considered a match for the German Army. Informed by the Minister of War, Hore Belisha, that they were the best-equipped fighting force ever to leave British shores, they set off with redundant First World War armoury to face the Luftwaffe and Rommel's 7th Panzer Division. These Highlanders became the sacrificial lambs of the doomed British Expeditionary Force.

Throughout that April and May of 1940 the 51st Highlanders meandered, apparently without direction, through Belgium and France, while Ostend, Ypres and Lille fell to the German advance and Hitler proclaimed a war of "total annihilation" against his enemies. "They kept moving us about," one man recalled. "They didn't seem to know what to do with us. Nobody really knew what was happening, at least in the ranks we never knew what was happening, and it's doubtful if our roll officers had a great idea of what was going on either."

By 27 May, with the bulk of the rest of the British Expeditionary Force – some half a million men – holed up on the expansive beaches of Dunkirk, the authorities had decided what to do with their Highland recruits. The men from the islands were sent to guard the Maginot Line to buy time, with their young lives, for an evacuation to take place. French tanks and the Highland Division, all under the command of General Charles de Gaulle, were strung out along the Somme from Abbeville to Amiens. For much of the time they were effectively behind German lines, telegraphing messages back to Headquarters in Gaelic to confuse the Germans who tapped the wires within a few miles of the British dugouts. "We didn't realise how poorly equipped we were," said one Uisteach later, "until we came up against the Germans. The equipment we had was just what they stopped using in 1918. Just one machine-gun per section, no Tommy-guns – even the French had Beretta Tommy-guns which we had to borrow. Our anti-tank gun was just like a pea-shooter, it would just stot off the German tanks."

After a week of death and chaos on the Maginot Line the evacuation of Dunkirk was complete and the Highlanders were ordered to retreat south to Le Havre. They marched down the coast as far as St Valery-en-Caux before Rommel's Panzers rumbled around from the south and surrounded 8,000 men. The crofters were reluctant to surrender – Rommel noted in his diary that this particular enemy "fought desperately . . . in spite of heavy fire the British troops did not give up". But at 10.30 on the morning of 12 June 1940 the war ended for the former Territorials from the southern isles. Ordered by their commanders to lay down their arms, many at first refused. Not knowing and not caring about the massive superiority of the enemy which encircled St Valery-en-Caux, they pleaded to be allowed to fight their way out. When finally they did lay down their weapons and belongings at their feet, there were tears of frustration and humiliation in their eyes. "It was the business of surrendering your arms, that is really where you came to the realisation of it, that here you were, your rifle was down there, your magazines were grounded and you were left as you stood. That was the realisation."

The 8,000 51st Highlanders were marched north to Belgium, through Holland and into Germany in the dry heat of a continental summer. They were escorted through a baying crowd to the central park of Dusseldorf and put on to barges for a three-day voyage down the Rhine. They were then crowded, 50 or 60 at a time, on to cattle-trucks and left standing for another three-day journey into the heart of darkest Europe, to the *of-lags* of occupied Poland. One or two escaped en route, one or two died from the privations of the journey, but for most, for a substantial number of the young men of the Uists and Benbecula, of Eriskay, Barra and Vatersay, five long years were about to be taken from their lives. The fact that two years later another, re-formed, 51st

Highland Division was to take its revenge upon Rommel on the desert sands of North Africa would be little comfort.

At home in the southern isles the news of the Fall of France and its consequences for their people sank in slowly. In so small a population the loss was disproportionately great, but the southern isles were used to that, and this time there was the consolation that, unlike the carnage which had ended 22 years previously, a substantial number of young men were, even if condemned to incarceration in a distant land, still alive.

The people of the southern isles in the Second World War did what they had done throughout the previous hundred years of fraction and assault – they stoically got on with their lives. Crofts were still worked, helped by the slow introduction of the tractor and by the establishment of a Food Production Committee in Lochboisdale, which was headed by a man from the Department of Agriculture, John Warnock, who had the power to exempt crofters – usually a husband with a family, or the eldest son of a widow – from military service. Women, as elsewhere in Britain, took the bulk of the work on themselves. Small boats put out into the various sounds throughout the summer months to tempt lobsters into home-made creels. The islands' situation, facing out to the troubled North Atlantic, left them both strangely close to, and disconnected from, the "phoney" sea war of 1939 and 1940: while telegraphic communication with the mainland was inexplicably cut in the early months of the war, the people of Barra and South Uist were able almost to watch as the aircraft carrier *Courageous* was attacked by U-Boats in the Inner Minch. Two units of the Home Guard were set up, one in South Uist and one in Barra. The commander of the first was Mr (later Captain) Finlay Mackenzie, the proprietor of the Lochboisdale Hotel; while that 56-year-old writer, Compton Mackenzie, who had settled by the Traigh Mhor, took charge in

Barra.

Mackenzie enjoyed a busy couple of years as Captain of the Barra Company of the 2nd Inverness-shire Battalion of the Home Guard, firing off cantankerous letters and newspaper articles complaining about the inadequacy of mail and tele-phonic communications, about the lack of tyres for his car – one of the few in Barra – and about the hilarious equipping of his men with pikes instead of rifles. The famous mock-alert of September 1940 left his command in Barra quite unmoved. While the signal CROMWELL, the code for INVASION STARTED, was being flashed from Harris to Lochboisdale (where "Finlay Mackenzie . . . led his warriors to the beaches prepared with thirty rifles to fling the enemy back into the sea") the Barra Home Guard hummed along, happily unaware, throughout a whole weekend until, on the Monday morning, Mackenzie received simultaneously the code word CROMWELL and the signal for ALL OVER.

Not surprisingly, Mackenzie began to consider a comic novel. A major character fell almost immediately into his lap. Aware of the self-esteem of the Barra doctor, a man named Samuel Bartlett, Mackenzie asked him to be an umpire in one of the unit's "invasion" exercises. "Unaware that it was I who had suggested him," Mackenzie remem-bered later, "[he] talked about the importance of his post and the wisdom of those who had realised it by appointing himself." Bartlett's subsequent umpiring consisted of little more than sustaining unwinnable arguments with local men as to whether they had been "shot" ("Well, anyway, you're both casualties." "And you're a casualty too," said Archie Maclean, aiming his rifle at the doctor). Mackenzie had a cast-list and a setting. Samuel Bartlett was about to receive unrequested immortality as Captain Paul Waggett of the

Great Todday Home Guard.

Evidence of the sea war, evidence which was hardly needed by a population with so many of its men serving in the merchant marine and the Royal Navy, was continuously being washed up on the islands' receptive shores. Some of that evidence was grisly. When the *Arandora Star,* a ship carrying German and Italian internees across the Atlantic to America, was sunk by U-boats in August 1940, many of the bodies, including that of a young guard, a Lovat Scout from Benbecula, were retrieved from the beaches of the southern isles and given a Catholic burial in their graveyards. A cargo vessel, the *Oak Crest,* was torpedoed 700 miles out into the North Atlantic four months later. An Irish seaman sailed 22 of his shipmates back east in a lifeboat. Eleven of them, including a young man from Barra, died of exposure before the Irishman grounded the boat on the west side of Barra at nightfall and then himself died on the shore. Of the 11 survivors, five more died overnight on the sand before the remainder were spotted and helped to safety.

Shortly after this, in December 1940, a barrel of rum from the doomed *Jamaica Queen* was washed up at Eoligarry in Barra. A Greek vessel, the *Eugenia Emberikos,* was wrecked on the east side of Barra in January 1942. Upon landing its captain promised the inhabitants of the island a formidable supply of retsina wine, ouzo, olives, cheese, cigarettes, coffee and figs, but overnight the ship was battered by heavy seas and broke in half, its treasury of foreign luxuries disappearing beneath the waves. The captain got ashore with one consolation: a skinny, black-faced sheep. And in January 1944 the *Samuel Dexter,* a liberty ship bringing wartime supplies to Britain, came to grief in the Sound of Barra, delivering 18,000 Camel cigarettes, tins of sweetcorn (which was fed to ungrateful island hens), gallon tins of tomato juice and four typewriters.

Cuile Mhoire, in wartime, was a bittersweet trove.

In 1940 the authorities began to build an aerodrome at the north of the southern isles, in the ancient Benbecula township of Balivanich. Its purpose at the time was simply to serve as a base for aircraft, such as Flying Fortresses, to pursue the war in the North Atlantic, although as the war progressed and its battlegrounds shifted eastwards the Balivanich landing strip was redundant almost before it was completed. But these things are not easily predicted in wartime and so the Air Ministry bought from the trustees of the Gordon Estate 3,000 acres of good Benbecula crofting land. Fifteen years later they acquired a further 1,700 acres in the neighbourhood and developed the whole scheme as a rocket firing range which was to change, irrevocably, the face of that quiet island. In the early 1940s the disruption brought about by the building of the aerodrome and landing strip was temporary. A few years earlier such enormous investment in the Outer Isles would have brought much-needed labouring work to local men. In wartime, with as much as one fifth of the male population at sea and many more serving in North Africa and stewing in Polish prison camps, labour had to be imported from the Scottish lowlands, from England and from neutral Ireland. These were thirsty workers and they were earning a substantial wage: up to ten pounds per week. But Balivanich did not, at the time, possess a public house.

On 4 February 1941 Donald MacAulay, the proprietor of a licensed premises near to Balivanich, the old staging inn at Creagorry, at the north end of the South Ford which separated Benbecula from South Uist, travelled to Askernish to learn from John MacDonald, who had been retained as factor of the estate by Lady Gordon Cathcart's Trustees, if there would be any objection to him building a bar in Balivanich. The following day

MacDonald replied to MacAulay by letter. "In connection with a canteen at the works at Balivanich," suggested MacDonald, "I now write to say that I do not anticipate any objection by the Trustees. I have written them on the matter and you may take it that they will be quite agreeable to your application to the licensing authority for a licence."

MacDonald and MacAulay were both sublimely ignorant, for the time being, of the cargo of the *bata mor* – the large ship which, earlier that very morning, a youth from South Glendale had spotted securely grounded on a reef in the Sound of Eriskay.

THREE

Sleek and Handsome Vessels

Thi tha chomhnadh nan ard,	*O Thou who pervadest the heights,*
Tiuirich duinn do bheannachd aigh,	*Imprint on us Thy gracious blessing,*
Iomchair leinn air bharr an t-sal,	*Carry us over the surface of the sea,*
Iomchair sinn gu cala tamh,	*Carry us safely to a haven of peace,*
Beannaich ar sgioba agus bat,	*Bless our boatmen and our boat,*
Beannaich gach acair agus ramh,	*Bless our anchors and our oars,*
Gach stadh is tarruinn agus rac,	*Each stay and halyard and traveller,*
Ar siuil-mhora ri crainn ard	*Our mainsails to our tall masts*
Cum a Righ nan dul 'n an ait	*Keep, O King of the elements, in their place*
Run 's gu 'n till sinn dachaidh slan	*That we may return home in peace*
. . . Gach la's oidhche, gach stoirm is fiamh,	*. . . Each day and night, storm and calm,*
Bi thusa leinn, a Thriath nan triath,	*Be Thou with us, O Chief of chiefs,*
Bi fein duinn ad chairt-iuil,	*Be Thou Thyself to us a compass-chart,*

Biodh do lamh air failm ar stiuir,	Be Thine hand on the helm of our rudder,
Do lamh fein, a Dhe nan dul,	Thine own hand, Thou God of the elements,
Moch is anamoch mar is iul,	Early and late as is becoming,
Moch is anamoch mar is iul.	Early and late as is becoming.
— *Beannachadh Cuain*	— *The Ocean Blessing*

The six sister cargo vessels which issued from the Teesside yards of the Furness Shipbuilding Company Limited, to the order of Furness, Withy & Co Ltd. London, between 1921 and 1923 were sleek, handsome vessels. Nobody could have anticipated, as they splashed into the calm waters which divide the North Riding of Yorkshire from the County of Durham, their boisterous careers.

They weighed in at almost 8,000 tons each but their single-screw steam turbines, supplied by John Brown of Clydebank, drove them along at up to 14 knots – an expensive speed, but a necessary investment for an ambitious merchant fleet. And the six ships were nothing if not ambitiously conceived. Their speed, comportment, and innovatory design – such as the positioning of crew accommodation amidships – attracted a great deal of interest in the early 1920s. The *London Commerce, London Importer, London Mariner, London Shipper, Manchester Regiment* and *London Merchant* – all christened by Furness Withy in celebration of one or another of their national business interests – had been built partly to help replace the merchant fleet which had been ravaged in the First World War, when more than 70 British cargo ships were sunk. It is ironic, then, that only two of this elegant sextuplet of low-slung, 450-foot shelter-deckers came to a peaceful end.

Those two were the *London Importer,* which served the Admiralty as a fleet supply ship, renamed the *Reliant,* during the

Second World War – she was later sold to a Maltese company and ended her working life trading for Pakistani owners as the *Firdausa*; and the *London Commerce,* which was bought by Liverpool's Harrison Lines in 1935, renamed *Collegian,* and scrapped in 1948.

The first to go violently was the *Manchester Regiment.* She was accidentally run down, with the loss of nine lives, by the liner *Oropesa* while in passage between Manchester and New Brunswick in December 1939. The *London Mariner,* which had also been bought by Thomas and James Harrison and renamed *Craftsman,* was captured and sunk by the German *Kormoran* in April 1941. One month later, on 17 May 1941, the *London Shipper,* by then sailing for Harrison Lines as the *Statesman,* bound for Belfast and Liverpool on a return voyage from New Orleans, was sunk with the loss of only one hand by a German aerial torpedo attack 200 miles west of Ireland. For the stylish sisters who had first split the water at Haverton-Hill-on-Tees 20 years earlier, 1941 was not a lucky year.

The adventures which attended the last weeks of the *London Merchant* entered the history books, but in fact her early career was fittingly rakish. Before her formal launch in August of 1923 she was run into and damaged by another vessel during her final fitting-out on the Tees. Repairs having been effected and her dignity soothed, she was sent with one of her sisters, the *London Shipper,* to ply between Vancouver and Panama. It was on this run that she had her first unhappy flirtation with hard liquor. The year was 1924 and Prohibition had been enforced in the United States of America for four years. This was not the case, of course, in Canada and Central America, but the *London Merchant* made the mistake of putting in at Portland, Oregon, with a cargo of whisky bound for the south, and thereby brought about an extraordinary international incident.

The liquor had in fact been approved, passed and sealed by the American Federal authorities but an enthusiastic Oregon State Prohibition Director overrode his superiors, broke their seal and seized the whole consignment. The *London Merchant's* master refused to leave the Columbia River without his full cargo, the British Embassy lodged a fierce complaint and the Federal authorities, embarrassed and annoyed by the Portland upstart, acted swiftly and sharply. The whisky was returned to the *London Merchant* and the Oregon State Prohibition Director was required to mollify the British Government and the Furness Withy shipping company by writing a full and grovelling apology.

The ship ploughed contentedly up and down the Pacific Ocean until the Christmas Eve of 1927, when she was involved in another slight collision. After repairs she ran between New York and Philadelphia until 1930 when, reined in by the creeping international depression, she was laid up with her sisters and no fewer than 60 other redundant cargo ships at Tollesbury on the River Blackwater. For five long years the *London Merchant* sat at anchor in the Essex marshes, looking out past Colne Point at the grey English Channel, until the May of 1935 when Furness Withy sold her to the Charente Steamship Company, a subsidiary of the Liverpool shipping line of Thomas and James Harrison. Charente renamed her the SS *Politician*.

For four years the *Politician* plied the sea routes of coastal Africa for Harrisons, running from Dakar, round the Cape of Good Hope, and putting in at Durban and Beira in the Ellerman and Clan trading service, breaking occasionally to navigate the more hectic lanes of the North Atlantic Ocean. At the outbreak of the Second World War, Harrisons were obliged to put her at the service of the Admiralty, and she embarked upon a brief and furious career in some of the most dangerous seas in the history of merchant shipping. Between September 1939 and the New

Year of 1941 the *Politician* steamed across the North Atlantic between Liverpool and Manchester and New Orleans and the West Indies on 11 occasions. Every hour of such a voyage in those momentous 15 months was accompanied by unprecedented hazard, and every voyage successfully completed was a massive boost to the British war effort.

Nobody who experienced the Battle of the Atlantic would be caught describing 1939 and 1940 as the years of the Phoney War. The first shots in a titanic struggle between British surface vessels and their invisible adversaries, the German High Command's *Unterseebooten,* or U-boats, were fired within hours of war being declared when the U30 sank without warning the British passenger liner *Athenia* in the North Atlantic. The codes of the sea battle were thus established, and its ground – the essential cargo-shipping lines between North America and Britain – determined.

Britain entered this battle sadly unprepared. The destroyer class of warship, which had been developed during the First World War to deal with the fledgling U-boat fleet, was reduced to 150 ships. The Germans had apparently only 48 operational submarines (although they promptly began to turn out more); but given that a good many of the British destroyers were necessarily committed to the Fleet, given the amount of British merchant shipping that had to cross the Atlantic if the nation was to survive and given that some destroyers were not as yet equipped with the submarine detection device ASDIC, that ASDIC was virtually ineffective against a U-boat on the surface of the water and that few ships were to have an effective radar system until the end of 1941, it is no surprise that the U-Boat commanders quickly slipped on, in their own country, the glamorous mantle of First World War air aces.

Throughout 1940 and into the early months of 1941 these undersea raiders, these "wolf-packs", enjoyed what they came to know as their "Happy Time". An enormous number of ships crossed the Atlantic carrying saleable merchandise to the markets of North America and bringing back crates of processed meat, preserved fish, and above all, armaments. In February 1941 the Canadian Navy Minister announced that in the whole of 1940 3,770 ships carrying dead-weight cargo tonnage amounting to 22,260,000 tons crossed from North America to Britain. There simply were not the ships of war available to escort them all, and so many went in unescorted convoys, or meagrely escorted convoys, or – like the *Politician* and her surviving sisters and many other of the faster vessels of the merchant marine – on an independently routed course, breaking from comparatively safe British waters to race, solo, for the American Security Zone.

The Fall of France in the May and June of 1940, that same catastrophe which sent so many Hebridean soldiers marching to captivity, also gave the Germans new ports from which to harry those soldiers' neighbours who were working the Atlantic trade routes. The carnage was extraordinary. Between July and October of 1940 alone 144 unescorted British ships were sent to the bottom of the sea, 73 more sunk while under the "protection" of ill-equipped convoys, and only two U-boats were put out of action. In the year between July 1940 and June 1941, 3,500,000 tons of British merchant shipping was sunk in the North Atlantic Ocean. This was the origin of the plentiful remains of cargo and of human beings which the Gulf Stream washed persistently up on to the shores of the southern isles of the Hebrides in those months. These were the months before the United States entered the war, even before she agreed to augment the British fleet by handing over, under the lease-lend agreement, a package of old but serviceable First World War destroyers. And the cruel truth was that at this time the great majority of shipping was torpedoed in the east of the North Atlantic, in the few hundreds of miles of sea which surrounds the Rockall Oceanic Bank, in the waters off the west coast of Ireland and Cornwall, sometimes as close to home as the Butt of Lewis, the Pentland Firth and the North Channel which separates Kintyre from Northern Ireland. Every merchant ship which left a British port for the North Atlantic at that time was playing short-odds Russian Roulette.

Captain Beaconsfield Worthington had heard the firing pin thump down on an empty barrel 11 times before he prepared his ship, the SS *Politician,* in Liverpool docks for another run in February 1941. Worthington was 63 years old and had almost 50 years at sea behind him. A west countryman from Plymouth, he had been something of a naval prodigy, gaining his master's certificate at Hull in 1903 at the age of 26. He was a stolid but not entirely humourless man who observed the proprieties of his own time by socialising privately only with senior officers while at sea. This was his second world war, his second spell of pitting his wits against U-boats, battleships and torpedo-carrying aircraft, and he was about to enter his seventh year as master of the *Politician*. He was held in high regard by the shipping companies and by the Admiralty. What was about to happen to Captain Beaconsfield Worthington would bear that out.

The voyage which the *Politician* was preparing to make, as Captain Worthington surveyed the busy Mersey docks from his bridge in the early days of February 1941, differed from her previous wartime runs in only a couple of apparently insignificant details. She was off to her familiar stamping-grounds of Kingston, Jamaica, and New Orleans. Her holds were filled with the usual hastily assembled miscellany of goods which might realise hard cash in the United States, and with essential items for the West Indian colonies. Cotton, machetes, flycatchers and confectionery; motorcycle hubs, enamelware and oil-burning stoves; cutlery, exercise books and plumbing equipment; cigarettes, tobacco, soap and medicines; carpets, baths, mirrors, pineapple cubes and biscuits. Despite the strange, colonial vagary of shipping *back* processed cotton, tobacco and pineapple to the West Indies, there was nothing out of the ordinary in the bulk of the *Politician's* cargo that February.

She did, however, have on board several cases which caused, for a number of years afterwards, a sheet which recorded their presence to be removed from the Customs file containing the ship's manifest, its bill of lading, and the details of its cargo. They were sensitive cases. Then and for years after the war the presses of the British company De La Rue turned out the printed currency for half of the countries of the world. These countries, which included Jamaica, required banknotes in wartime as they had in peacetime, and so the *Politician* had stowed away, at the request of Greenshields, Cowie & Co Ltd., Crown Agents for the Colonies, eight cases of Jamaican ten shilling, one pound and five pound notes. They occupied a space in Hold Number Five measuring 29 feet by four feet. Their value was approximately £3 million.

But it was the rest of the contents of Hold Number Five which would make the SS *Politician* famous. In the winter of 1940–41 German bombing raids on the industrial heart of the Scottish lowlands, the plains of the Forth and the Clyde, had succeeded in causing great damage to two warehouses, one in Leith and one in Glasgow, which were storing whisky. After the establishment of the wartime Coalition Government in Britain a new Secretary of State for Scotland, a socialist Member of Parliament named Tom Johnston, moved to export as much of Scotland's unique golden treasury as possible before further damage was done. An enormous quantity of top-quality whisky was gathered from Scotland's chief distillers. From John Walker

& Sons, James Buchanan, Distillers, Haig & Haig, Peter
Mackenzie, James Martin, Ballantine's and a select band of
others, a formidable array of above-average proof, malted and
blended, bottled, casked, cartoned and crated whisky was
collected, transported to Liverpool docks, and cached in the SS
Politician, mostly in the ship's Number Five Hold, just aft of the
engine and boiler rooms, directly above the main shaft tunnel
which housed her powerful single screw.

The equivalent of 22,000 cases, or 264,000 bottles, of whisky
was loaded onto the *Politician* that February. It was bound for
the American "millionaire market" and its brand names were
beyond parody. Liverpudlian stevedores hauled aboard crates of
The Antiquary, Haig's Pinch, VVO Gold Bar, Ballantine's
Amber Concave, White Horse, King's Ransom, Victoria Vat,
Johnnie Walker Red and Black Label, Mountain Dew, King
William IV, McCallum's Perfection, King George IV, PD
Special, Old Curio and Spey Royal. Added, almost irrelevantly,
to this regal haul were 90 crates of stout and 60 of sherry.

And not one bottle, case or crate bore the Excise stamp. The
drink was for export only: not a penny of duty had been paid on
a single drop of it. On sale in New Orleans and Texas it was
expected to net up to half a million pounds.

Ordinarily Captain Beaconsfield Worthington would not
have taken his ship from Liverpool to Kingston and New
Orleans by way of the Minch, the Inner Hebridean Sea which
separates the Outer Isles from Skye and the mainland. But those
were not ordinary times: his orders from the Admiralty were to
proceed independently on their route instructions. The logic
behind the Admiralty's route instructions was to take him as far
north and west as possible in reasonably protected waters, and
then for him to turn on the power of his still speedy vessel, nip
through the islands and make a break for the Americas.

By dusk on 3 February 1941, Captain Beaconsfield Worthington had been informed by his Mate, a Londoner named R. A. Swain, that 51 men had signed on and only one, a fireman, had failed to join the ship. At seven o'clock on the following morning the crew began to prepare for sea. By eight o'clock Mr Swain reported a light wind and clear weather, and at 9.09 anchors were weighed and the *Politician* proceeded on her last voyage. At 9.15 the crew attended boat drill, donned lifebelts, and Mr Swain checked the security of the outboard lifeboats. At 10.32 the Mersey Channel was cleared, the Bar Lightship appeared to port, the pilot left and in fine, clear, breezy weather the boat steamed quickly up to and past the Isle of Man, through the North Channel and towards the Hebrides.

By eight o'clock that evening the breeze had turned into a moderate wind, the sky had turned cloudy and a slight swell was getting up. At midnight on 4 February rain was beginning to fall, the wind had become fresh and the sea moderate. A new course was fixed here, in the disturbed waters which separate the seaboard of the Scottish Gaidhealtachd from the coasts of Antrim, Londonderry and Donegal. It was aimed to take the *Politician* to a position ten miles west of the famous Skerryvore Light. From there she should have been able to fix another position from the Barra Head Light and negotiate safe entry to the Minch. This was a time-honoured sea-going manoeuvre. However, the *Politician* was neither the first nor the last to get it wrong.

At four o'clock on the morning of 5 February Mr Swain made his last entry, while at sea and under way, in the deck log-book of the SS *Politician*. The wind, he recorded, was south-westerly. There was a gale blowing and a rough sea. The night was overcast and it was raining. Eight minutes later the vessel's course was altered again, for the last time. There is no record of

Skerryvore or Barra Head Lights, whose high walls were painted black during the war, having been sighted, but for three hours and 30 minutes the *Politician* steamed in a roughly accurate direction, N 29 E compass, making N 13 E true.

At 7.40 a.m., precisely 57 minutes before the end of the official blackout in wartime Inverness-shire, all hell broke out on the SS *Politician*.

The shallows of the Sound of Eriskay really begin to the west of Calvay Island, a large rock to the east of the sound. There, the low tide depth of the sea reduces suddenly and enormously, from between 20 and 30 feet to two, three and four feet – from the sort of depth in which a ship the size of the *Politician* might make water, to one in which it would have no chance. But at this stage in its Hebridean adventure the *Politician* did not venture into the shallows of the Sound of Eriskay. Nor, as has been suggested, did she strike the Island of Calvay, or the rocks off the coast of South Uist. Roughly half a mile south-east of Calvay, just off Rosinish Point on Eriskay, a lozenge of rock and sandbanks rises wickedly up from the bed of the sea. These banks never break the surface of the water and on a wet, dark night are quite invisible. They have no name.

At 7.40 on the morning of 5 February the bridge of the *Politician* learnt that their course was slightly awry. The lookout watch, which consisted of two experienced seamen, neither of whom had previously served on the *Politician,* and one 16-year-old apprentice, suddenly signalled "Land ho!".

The land was five to six points to the starboard bow and it was looming massively towards them. It was, in fact, Ru Melvich, a 350-foot outcrop of rock, uninhabited and miles from any settlement, without a light or other forewarning, which bludgeons into the Little Minch and forms the southerly reach of the island of South Uist.

Mr Swain desperately swung the helm hard-a-port and put the engines full astern. The *Politician* might yet have been saved if it had not been for that hidden, nameless bank of rock and sand. Losing forward momentum quickly, she lurched on to it, her bow rose briefly into the air, and then she settled down with a dreadful, calamitous rumble.

It was still only 7.45. Captain Beaconsfield Worthington had reached the bridge and was becoming increasingly aware of the awfulness of his predicament. No U-boat had struck. There had been no attack from the surface of the sea or from the air. The men on the bridge of the SS *Politician* had simply miscalculated their position.

The oil fuel tanks which lay along the keel of the ship had been smashed during the grounding and water and oil was flooding, not only Holds Number One, Five and Six, but also the engine-room itself. After 20 minutes Chief Engineer Mossman, a 55-year-old Liverpudlian with lengthy experience of the *Politician,* gave up the unequal struggle. The order was still coming down from the bridge to keep engines hard astern, but the ship, far from floating, was making no headway at all, and Mr Mossman's working quarters were quickly flooding. At five past eight he signalled above "Finished with engines". Grimly, Mr Swain noted the fact in the deck log and added, almost automatically, as if such things were likely ever to bother the *Politician* again, "Whole gale rain. Squally."

In the 50 years that have followed there has been much speculation about the reasons for the *Politician* grounding herself north-east of Eriskay. It has been suggested that she simply took the wrong turning in the night, mistaking the unnavigable Sound of Eriskay for the Sounds of Mingulay, Sandray, Pabbay or even of Barra in her dash for the open sea. But Mr Swain's deck log proves conclusively that there was no intention to veer to port south of Ru Melvich; that manoeuvre was made only to avoid the looming rock. It has been suggested that the crew was drunk but there is no evidence of that from people who knew Swain and Worthington; both were reportedly responsible and reliable officers. It has been suggested that the compass itself was dizzy, affected by magnetite in the gabbro rock formations of the Outer Isles. But the fact is that none of the above were necessary to bring a boat to grief in these waters, in peacetime or in war. They are not easy seas to navigate and their complexity is compounded by the severity of local tidal forces. Just three days later, on 8 February, the SS *Thala* went aground within a mile of the *Politician,* and her 35 survivors had to be shipped to Tobermory. In 1940 the *Birchol* was wrecked on the south end of South Uist. Since human beings first began to navigate, ships have suffered greater or lesser damage in the seas of the Hebrides. The *Politician,* for all her subsequent fame, was just another casualty in a list longer than Lloyd's Registry.

One thing at least is certain: Messrs Worthington and Swain did not have a clue as to where they were when dawn broke on that February morning. Their first distress signal, picked up by Port Patrick Radio in the Rhinns of Galloway on Scotland's south-west coast, immediately the ship found herself in trouble, stated: "Abandoning ship. Making water. Engine-room flooded." The second, logged at Plymouth at 8.22 a.m., put the *Politician's* position as "Ashore south of Barra Island, pounding heavily". The nearest naval vessel was the HMS *Abelia,* and at 10.25 she requested of the Admiralty: "Which side of Barra Island, east or west?" Neither the Admiralty nor the radio officer on board the SS *Politician* could advise the *Abelia* on this point, and at 10.45 a.m. she signalled back, helplessly: "Cannot make west side Barra Island daylight will investigate. Distress indefinite did not state east or west."

On board the *Politician,* ten full nautical miles north of either side of Barra, things were moving by that time. At 10.30 both anchors had been dropped. The unpopulated eastern coasts of both South Uist and Eriskay had come more clearly into view as the day had broken and the mist began to rise. Captain Worthington still considered that there was a serious danger of his vessel breaking up completely in the heavy swell and so 26 non-essential members of the crew – stewards, cooks and galley boys – were put aboard Lifeboat Number Four and lowered into the fierce sea.

Unknown to its crew, Number Four Lifeboat was being watched by bright, interested eyes as it swept impotently towards the coast of South Uist. Schoolboy Duncan MacInnes had arrived a little earlier at Rosinish Point on Eriskay, in the company of a friend, to be greeted by a spectacular sight. He remembered many years later:

There she was, lying battered by mountainous seas from the south-east, stern-on to the wind and facing the Uist coastline. It was some ship, what they call an intermediate, with black funnel, buff goal-posts and fully seven hatches. The blade hull looked enormous sitting so high out of the water at low tide. I got there to see quite a number of people already down to gaze on the big Harrison liner.

About 10.30 a.m. a number of seamen, all in white jackets, scrambled aboard one of the port lifeboats. This seemed to us a very silly thing to do because they were quite safe, but of course they didn't know that at the time . . . They manned the boat and managed to unship the falls and let her drift, only to be battered by the huge seas. Oars would have been pointless in any case that day, although one steering oar would have been useful.

We watched spellbound till the tiny vessel disappeared in
the foam and fury of the cliff-face at Rubha Dubh. Then, just
as we began to think the worst, a miracle happened, when the
[men] were flung on the shore.

On board the *Politician,* whose radio room was still under
crackling siege from the Admiralty to offer a precise location –
the Barra lifeboat had set off south half-an-hour earlier, and the
dogged *Abelia* was still steaming hopefully towards Castlebay –
little could be done except pray for their colleagues, shipwrecked,
apparently upon some deserted Hebridean shore. Over on
Eriskay the response was more helpful. Men sprinted from
Rosinish Point over to the island's anchorage at Haun. A sailing-
boat was put under way and with a virtuosity which astonished
the merchant seamen watching from the decks of the *Politician*
it negotiated the Sound of Eriskay, put in at the perilous rocks
of Rubha Dubh, landed the 26 sailors and took them back to
Eriskay.

Captain Worthington and Mr Swain were thus made aware
that they were within reach of human habitation. But they were
no nearer to knowing exactly *where*. At 11.13 a.m. the Navy sent
the *Salvonia* out of Greenock on the Clyde to look for the
Politician in the vicinity of Vatersay. At three minutes to noon
the *Abelia* was told yet again by the Admiralty that, in answer to
her earlier query, the cargo ship's last known position had been
south of Barra.

By one o'clock in the afternoon Captain Worthington was
growing more confident about the condition of his vessel.
Soundings of the hull as the morning had progressed indicated
that the water level was not rising, the weather was moderating
and the *Politician* had not broken in two or slipped under the
waves. At six minutes past one in the afternoon he ordered his

radio officer to transmit: "Engine-room flooded. Salvage possible if assistance of tugs and pumps sent immediately." Unfortunately, Captain Worthington preceded this message with the words: "*Politician*. Ashore Barra Sound."

This was closer. The Sound of Barra is north, not south of that island. But it is not the Sound of Eriskay. Captain Worthington finally learned that the island to his north was not Barra or Eriskay, but South Uist, and that to his south was not Vatersay or Barra, but Eriskay, at three o'clock that afternoon when, with the wind and seas abating, the sailing-boat which had collected his capsized men from the shores of Rubha Dubh arrived from Eriskay to deliver them back to him.

At 4.45 p.m. the Barra lifeboat, having spent the previous six and three-quarter hours trawling fruitlessly about between Castlebay and Barra Head, arrived alongside the *Politician*. The crew, some of them white and shaken, some cheerful, one or two with the tops of bottles showing out of their coat pockets, gratefully scrambled aboard and were taken to Barra for the night.

Twenty hours later, at 12.45 on the following afternoon, Port Patrick Radio issued a further broadcast. It said: "Ship lying most easterly point of Eriskay Island, South Uist, Outer Hebrides."

When Captain Worthington reported that his ship was salvable the Admiralty took him at his word. On the following morning of 6 February Coxswain Murdo MacNeil took the captain and Mr Swain and some of the crew back to their ship in the Castlebay lifeboat. They found, as Mr Swain reported in the deck log, the "situation unchanged". The crewmen loaded their shipmates' baggage on to two of the *Politician*'s lifeboats and these were towed back to Castlebay by the Barra lifeboat. On the tenth of the month all but 20 of the crew – senior officers and essential personnel – left Lochboisdale for Liverpool to be discharged.

Meanwhile, the directors of the Harrison Line and the *Politician*'s insurers, or underwriters, had been doing sums. The *Politician* was insured with a number of different companies to the total value of £196,000 (this excluded her wireless apparatus, which Marconi International Marine Communications Company eventually bought back for £37.19s.2d). The underwriters were faced with the ancient dilemma of houses meddling in high-risk capital – and the history of commerce has known few higher risks than insuring an independently routed British merchantman in 1941 – whether to draw a deep breath and write the whole thing off, or to order a thorough salvage and risk throwing good money after bad.

They asked the Liverpool and Glasgow Salvage Association, who were at the time official Admiralty agents, to inspect the vessel. At 10.30 on the morning of Saturday, 8 February, the Association's chief salvage officer, Commander Kay, boarded the *Politician* and carried out a survey. He found that the water level in most of the flooded holds was stable, and after leaving the ship for Lochboisdale at 4.30 p.m. he informed his superiors that salvage was feasible.

Incredibly, no sooner had Kay left the stricken liner that wet and squally afternoon than another merchant ship, the SS *Thala*, which was running at the head of a convoy of seven other ships with an escort of two corvettes and was loaded with iron ore, hit a rock off Hartamul, less than a mile south-east of the *Politician*. The *Thala*'s sirens trumpeted alarm and warning to her fellows; her crew was taken off; and on the following day she broke in half and slowly slid into the arms of the Minch.

On 10 February Harrison Lines and the underwriters, encouraged by Commander Kay's report, struck a deal with the

Salvage Association. They agreed to pay up to £5,000 regardless of success rate for "reasonable expenditure", and if Commander Kay's men brought up an acceptable quantity of goods, or even managed to refloat the vessel, "an award to be fixed by negotiation or arbitration" would be handed over.

On 11 February the first attempt to salvage the *Politician* and her cargo began. The salvage steamer *Ranger* arrived at her side, escorted from Ireland by PC 74. For some days the weather made it impossible to board the ship, but on 15 February Commander Kay and his divers, assisted by the *Politician's* remaining crew, managed to get on deck and make preliminary explorations. On 16 February they returned to connect steam pipes between the *Ranger* and the ship's derrick hoisters and took off a quantity of mail, which was handed over to the local post office, and some cargo. On 18 February the coaster *Corteen* arrived and the discharge of the cargo of the SS *Politician* commenced in earnest.

Commander Kay's first salvage of the contents of the ship was an admirably thorough operation in all but one respect. He took off everything he could, except for alcoholic liquids. He simply ignored the whisky and the stout and the sherry, presumably considering undutied, damaged cases of spirits, which were now floating in an unpleasant compound of oil and water, to be worthless.

Between 18 and 22 February Commander Kay loaded aboard the *Ranger* and the *Corteen* goods to the value of £38,340. He took off ten undamaged crates of boots and shoes, seven crates of enamelware, one keg of carbonate of magnesia and two, slightly damaged, bags of clover seed. Thirty-two bundles of toilet soap were duly lifted into the *Corteen,* along with eight drums of disinfectant, a bundle of plumbing pipes, two trusses of carpeting and three (damaged) baths. Hardly an item on the ship's manifest was left aboard, other than the whisky and the Jamaican banknotes. Unless it was for personal use, Commander Kay's men did not touch the whisky or the money.

The crew of the *Politician* spent 23 and 24 February dismantling her gun, the single safeguard that could be allowed her during a crossing of the beleaguered North Atlantic. Commander Kay had decided that the damage to the ship's hold was simply too extensive, she would never see New Orleans again. He reported back that while a reasonable quantity of undamaged cargo could be and had been removed, it was impractical to consider refloating the ship. On 24 February Harrison Lines, acting on advice relayed to them from the Liverpool and Glasgow Salvage Association, notified the 24 underwriters that the *Politician* was to be abandoned. Commander Kay and the *Ranger* stayed on until 12 March, diligently hauling out cases of glazed tiles and machetes, when they too considered the operation completed and steamed off to Glasgow's Springfield Quay with their salved cargo.

Two days before he left, Commander Kay had been asked by local customs officers, who were already nervous about the quantity of undutied whisky which remained on board the *Politician* and who were in receipt of worrying evidence that some of it had already found its way ashore, if it would be possible to leave a guard behind on the ship. Kay told them firmly that it would be unsafe and foolhardy. Secure as the tilting *Politician* appeared to be in calm weather, a sea change or an equinoctial gale could at any time break up the vessel and send her into the bitter sound, along with anybody who happened to be on board at the time. Commander Kay might have added that he saw no reason to waste anybody's time by putting them in charge of an abandoned ship and her cargo.

Disgruntled by Kay's unhelpful attitude, the customs men had to content themselves with climbing aboard the *Politician*, closing Hold Number Five and stamping upon it the official seal of the Commissioners of His Majesty's Customs and Excise, much as an innocent may ward off vampires by holding up a head of garlic.

That seemed to be the end of the matter. It was certainly the end of the SS *Politician* for Captain Beaconsfield Worthington, although not of his misfortunes in that cruel sea war. He became the master of a 7,000-ton cargo vessel, the SS *Arica*. On 6 November 1942, while sailing from London to Demerara, the *Arica* was sunk by U160, an *Unterseeboot* commanded by one of the heroes of the German submarine fleet, Lieutenant Georg Lasser. Twelve of the *Arica*'s crew lost their lives, but Worthington and 54 others landed safely at Trinidad on the following day. He died, in his bed, at the age of 84.

Like Worthington, Mr Swain was cleared of all blame by the official inquiry which followed. He went on to command another Harrison Lines ship, the *Custodian,* and he also survived the war.

Chief Engineer Mossman was to be down among the oil and water of a flooding hull one more time. In December 1942, while serving on the *Barrister,* he found himself going on to the rocks at Dingle Bay in the south-west of Ireland. "Well, I don't know," he is reputed to have commented, "we've done it again . . ."

For these men the affair of the *Politician* was over. For the people of the southern isles of the Outer Hebrides in that fine March of 1941, it was only just beginning.

FOUR

The King's Ransom

It was a case of doing your business during the night, when it was dark and nobody could see you on the run with the bicycle.
— Uist man

In truth, the people of the southern isles took little or no account of the niceties of the salvage laws. They were not used to applying to the authorities for relaxation of Section 536 of the Merchant Ship Act (1894), which prohibited the removal of the cargo of stranded ships, each time a hatchway door or a can of sweetcorn or a barrel of rum rolled up on their shore. They were not wreckers and they did not look to the sea to make them rich, but the items of use or luxury which it occasionally swept their way were small bonuses to a people who had lost so much to the sea. Its provender was *Cuile Mhoire,* and to take it home was to save it. The vocabulary which came to be used by players in the drama of the *Politician* is instructive. While customs officers talked of theft, plunder and looting, nobody from the southern isles ever talked of anything other than "saving" or "rescuing" the ship's cargo. The implications of the words "stealing" and "vandalism" were deeply offensive to these people, who were simply engaged in preserving, and putting to good use, the remainder of a condemned cargo from the Minch. The fact that the cargo was warmly welcomed by them, and was to prove deeply sensitive in some official quarters, was incidental.

It is also true that Commander Kay, when he called a close to his salvage operation on 12 March, and the Harrison Lines when they officially abandoned the ship to the elements on 24 February, had indicated with some clarity that they had no further interest in the SS *Politician* or in her residual oil-stained cargo. They seemed at the time to be willing to let her lie until she slipped, like so many others before her, rusted and broken into the sea.

Men from the islands had been up to and aboard the *Politician* from the first day of her grounding, when an Eriskay sailing-boat had rescued those 26 of her crew from the unhealthy shore at Rubha Dubh and delivered them safely back to Captain Worthington. Some had helped, as freelance labour, with Commander Kay's salvage. Many had tasted the fruits of her cargo, brought ashore by themselves or by her stranded crew. Some had taken an occasional trip out to her when Kay's men and Worthington's crew were landlocked by bad weather.

But the first wholesale rescuing of the cargo of the boat which was quickly and affectionately dubbed the *Polly* – a cognomen which as the weeks passed came to be applied not just to the parent vessel, but to all of her marvellous ingredients, as in a "bottle of Polly" – began only after the departure of the *Ranger*. By then the ship's fame had spread. Small boats began to arrive from all of the islands of the Hebrides and the western seaboard. These were the ketches and cobles in which the young men of the islands and the seaboard of the Gaidhealtachd still perfected their unique seamanship. They were, technically, small fishing smacks, often with just a single mast and sail, occasionally with two, usually between 15 and 20 feet long, making unladen just a few inches of water; sturdy, clinker-built, carefully tended and with a life expectancy that could be as long as or longer than that of a man. They were an essential part of the Hebridean economy. They were not only used for what fishing remained to the islands, but also for transporting animals to offshore grazings, and for making social trips – often of extraordinary distances – up and down the coast. They were quickly convertible to rowing skiffs in unsuitable weather for sailing, and in the March of 1941 they congregated at the SS *Politician* like a regatta.

From Mull, Skye, Lewis, Harris, Mallaig, Kyle, Oban and Gairloch the small boats arrived. "You would see people you hadn't seen in years," commented one man, comparing the gathering to the "Hielanman's Umbrella", the railway bridge in Glasgow's Argyle Street under which exiled Gaels assembled in cheerful company. You would also see boats you hadn't seen in years. On one occasion the *St Brendan,* which had been sold from South Uist to Gairloch in 1914 and had since changed hands again in Skye, arrived back in her native waters with a man from Lewis at the helm. "I'd know her anywhere," said an Eriskay fisherman, "she's the sister boat of mine, the *St Patrick*. Look at the slight difference in her hull . . ."

But for all of the social whirl, work in the holds of the *Politician* was generally a sober, diligent affair. "There wasn't much noise going on while we were probing for the whisky," remembered Norman MacMillan of Kilphedar in South Uist:

> There was plenty of light among the cargo, there was tons of candles, even Tilley lamps, and the place was well lit. It was like some sort of shrine, you know, and looked like it too, everybody so quiet and conscientious, digging for whisky there. But once they started to haul it up on to the top deck, when the tide came in, there was a good enough noise then.

"Heave!" "Lower!", shouting all the time! There were boats of every size and description there. We hardly dare talk once we got into them, but the good spirit always kept us afloat!

One local man, Angus John Campbell of Lochboisdale, had been boatswain on the Politician between the wars. "I knew my way about!" he would laugh later, and Duncan MacInnes, the boy who had watched the ship founder from Rosinish Point on the first day of her grounding, recalls arriving on her to find "a little boat from Lochboisdale already there". Angus John already had the locking bars off Hold Number Five, and upon seeing the Eriskay men called out: "Come, gentlemen, and join the party!" The adults with them, Duncan MacInnes recalled how they:

> boarded the vessel and went straight to Number Five, leaving us young fellows on the *St Winifred* under strict instructions not to follow. But temptation got the better of us, and we started up the Jacob's ladder. Eventually we made it to the deck and took a good breather after the perilous ascent in the fierce wind.
>
> We could see torches moving down in Number Five and a young man from Lochboisdale on guard over a single tea chest at the hatch. At first he was not very talkative, but we finally got round him and set off with him on a tour of the ship. We came across the lovely piano in the dining saloon. Everyone began to enjoy themselves, but I began to wonder about the tea chest, and leaving my friends to the music I doubled back.
>
> Picking up an empty sack from the deck, I approached the box, and without stopping to see what was inside, I started to help myself. With a length of shirting tied on to the sack I

lowered my haul into the boat, letting the material drop in after it. Then I returned to join my pals and we bade farewell to our friend from Lochboisdale before scrambling back on board the *St Winifred* to examine our booty.

We had nine bottles of McCallum whisky, a number of sandals or leather slippers, and an electric iron – which was useless to us as there was no electricity on the island.

Once the whisky had been taken home, to shoreside houses or distant crofts, it was considered politic, even from the early days, to bury or otherwise hide what had not been consumed or shared out. Norman MacMillan recalled:

You would do your best to get it undercover at home before night was out, and if you couldn't do that you had to cache it somewhere, to hide it 'til darkness came again. You dug a square hole somewhat as you would dig a grave, but with a little more care. You'd turn the turf back and carry the soil that you'd taken out of the hole as far away from the scene as possible. Then you rolled the turf back and you put a mark on it: the corner of a rock and a bit of iris and a bit of bullrush or something . . .

Bottles were thrust, cork end down, into the huge stacks of peat that stood by every house. They were pushed into rabbit holes and stored beneath stooks of hay. They were lowered in creels to the bottom of the sea, and they were piled neatly behind the pine-clad walls of living-rooms. Every available foot of furtive storage was used by a people who knew every square inch of their native lands.

At times it seemed almost that the islands would run out of hiding places. John MacPherson, the "Coddy", a good friend in

Barra of Compton Mackenzie and the folklorist John Lorne Campbell, was a famous reliquary of southern island song and story, and the time of the *Politician* added greatly to his repertoire. He was, in the years that followed, to tell many tales of those halcyon days, tales of sickly stirks being cured by the whisky and of old ladies who bathed their feet in "Polly" to ease rheumatism. To illustrate the congested condition of the natural storage space in the small island of Eriskay during 1941, the Coddy told Campbell the story of a man named Ronald . . .

. . . a fisherman and a very good one. Like many other Eriskay men – and more than Eriskay men – he was a famous hand at the *Polly*. In fact, he had tremendous stock in hand when the rumours came that an invasion of Excise officers were on the road to Eriskay. And he said to his wife, "Well, Catriona, we had better get the whisky out of the house," he says, "because the Excisemen are coming."

"Oh yes," said Catriona, "for God's sake take it away and don't let me see a drop of it coming into the house again. I am not getting a wink of sleep since it came into the house whatever, and you should have put it away long ago."

Now in the twilight this certain night Ronald filled a sugar bag which would contain three or four cases, and he put the whole show on his back, and he made an attempt to move his stock out of the house and hide it in the hill. Ronald was very tired of the bag before he reached his destination, and when he made himself believe that he was in the safest spot in Eriskay for hiding the lot, he let go the bag and emptied it all out.

Now next he got hold of a bottle and he tried to hide it into the corner of a rabbit burrow – and lo and behold, what happened, it struck against another one! Well, he tried it not far from the same place, and the same thing happened, and for six occasions in succession: Ronald could not get his bottle into a burrow because there was one there before him. So he gave up the ghost and returned to the dump, and he was admiring the bottles there and was going to bid them good night for ever, because tomorrow they would belong to someone else.

Then he saw on the side of the bottle, "The King's Ransom", and, "Well, I will see no more of those bottles," says Ronald, "and I think I will take a dram out of the King's Ransom" – so that Ronald did.

The medicine began to feel happy on Ronald, and he decided on taking another one, and at that one he sat down and treated himself to a smoke. And he said, "Ah well, I am very disappointed to be going away and leaving all these bottles behind – I think I'll take another dram." So that was number three. And so on. Continuing at that rate the bottle was very nearly empty before Ronald said to himself, "I had better go home", so he made for the homeward journey. And I'm telling you, he was making much better way on the outward journey! And crawling from port to starboard he was in a merry state – or perhaps a poor state.

It was twilight, and the wife could see Ronald coming home and she was wondering what was the matter with him and when he came closer she discovered that he was much the worse from the expedition to hide the "Polly". And she rolled out in Gaelic, "*Raghnaill, Raghnaill, dé tha ceàrr ort, a m'eudail?*" (Oh Ronald, Ronald, what is the matter with you, my dear?)

And Ronald said, "You know, Catriona, I took with me to the hill a big bag and I was certainly dead tired before I got it there. On arriving at the place where I was going to hide the bottles not a damn corner was there but there was a bottle in every burrow before me. And I drank the biggest part of one myself and now, supposing all the Excisemen between this and Hell itself comes, I would not go another inch to Ben Stack" – and Ronald went to bed.

And the next day, when he took a walk to admire the scenery he left yesterday, the coast was swept – there was nothing there.

On that occasion, the Excisemen may not have been responsible for removing Ronald's hoard. When the draconian crackdown was applied by the authorities the people of the southern isles did resent it and were fearful of it. But at least they were able to tell themselves that these eager officials were merely doing what they saw to be their job. No such excuse was allowable to the few who stole from the neighbours' stock. "I didn't mind so much the Customs getting it, for that was their duty," Duncan MacInnes said later. "What I did mind were the people who hadn't the courage to board the steamer yet fared as well as the ones who got themselves tired and oily. They would watch where we buried the stuff and unearth it later on." This was the first bad taste to issue from the unstopped bottles of the *Politician's* cargo, and it lingers in the mouths of some to the present day.

But the cargo, and therefore the haul, was not only whisky. Houses in the islands were curtained with the linen that was not used on board in makeshift hoists. Bicycle parts were eagerly sought after. Baths were put into houses with no running water and telephone equipment installed where there was no electricity. One man removed a sack of shoes, shipped them ashore and walked four miles home with them only to discover that they were all left-footed.

The whisky merely heightened the happy experience. Wonderful stories were told of its lack of toxicity – "You could drink it all day and all night and you would never have a headache after it . . . we always think it over, especially when we feel a bit dry . . ." – and there is little doubt that for many it offered a gay, blurred and welcome time out of war. "It was just one long continuous booze," remembered Norman MacMillan, "for six weeks. You didn't go to bed because as soon as you went to bed somebody would come hammering at the door that either had five bottles or he'd be asking for three . . ."

Those few cheerful, unhindered weeks at the *Polly* were, in fact, one big Rabelaisian harvest, with all of its associated hard work, dirt, risk and celebration. Donald Hector McNeil of Garynamonie in South Uist remembered clearly the unrefined gaiety of the occasion:

> She was dirty with tar and oil. We had to go up on that ladder which was against her side – it was so slippery you couldn't get a proper foothold, and grabbing it was just as difficult – but we got into her anyway.
>
> There was another ladder going down from the twin deck, down to the hold. You couldn't see the cases, they were under the oil, "Black oil on the surface – *ola dbubh gu h'ard*", as the saying goes, and you couldn't see one case, you had to clear the oil away. There was a long plank with something attached to it and all we were doing was to hit the cases with this and it was bringing them up to the surface.
>
> Someone then grabbed them and we got them up with ropes and other things. One night we landed 37 cases at Ludag. All we did then was to go home to get the carts – that was what we had then – every cart, and each one carrying up to 14 cases. We divided the spoil in Moclan Iain's house, we probably got seven cases each that night . . .
>
> There was another time we were down in the hold and doing very well. We were standing on a hatch in the hold and

grabbing the cases as they came to the surface. Alastair Iacain and myself were on the hatch and another came along and he was wanting to stand on the hatch as well. He stood on the other end, the hatch tipped, and we went skiting down – God knows where – right down into the depths. It seemed bottomless, but we managed to surface, and we were as black as a mound of tar.

Someone grabbed me. I think it was Angus John from Boisdale, and I was so slippery, so heavy with boots and oilskin, but he got his hands under my arms and pulled me in. Someone else was shouting, "Grab *me,* anyway! Grab *me!*" I was clinging to something and I felt like saying, "I'm all right, Jack!" So I was, as long as I had a hold of something. But I couldn't speak – oil was in my mouth. Anyway, it all turned out fine.

That night I walked four miles from Ludag home to get the horse and cart. My feet were really sore by the time I reached home, chafed and everything. I went into the byre and the horse nearly went through the wall seeing me so black. When I spoke to him and gave him a sheaf of oats he understood who I was. I couldn't wash myself properly, but I scraped away some of the grease. I returned with another boy from the village to Ludag and we took the cases back home later on that night.

The dreaded oil cost many a man his working clothes. Some would try to clean it off with the spoiled linen on board, others found useless Jamaican banknotes in a corner near to Number Five Hold and used these as hand- and face-towels, smearing the terrible stuff from their face and hands on to the loose currency before throwing handfuls of it away, overboard or down into the hold. A few, a very few, took samples of the money home. One or two of these were observed to have greater quantities than others. But most were interested in removing the oil. As time progressed, though, so the significance of the erstwhile contents of the *Politician*'s fuel tanks assumed greater proportions. From being an otherwise harmless ruiner of decent trousers, that oil would come to represent evidence which could send a man to jail.

Not everything of value and quality was rescued from the *Politician*. When word reached Donald Campbell, the school-teacher in Eriskay, of the beautifully inlaid little German piano that Duncan MacInnes had found in the ship's dining saloon, he applied to the authorities for permission to save it, assuring them that the Eriskay fishermen had agreed to ship it to dry land, free of charge. The authorities refused. Annoyed, Campbell wrote to that influential, campaigning author in Barra, Compton Mackenzie, asking for his help. Mackenzie, also, was refused permission. He was to claim later that Campbell's letter was the first he had heard of the wrecked cargo ship.

But the whisky got everywhere. Compton Mackenzie himself, who was appraised of the larger nature of the contents of the ship's holds by his neighbours on Barra, by men such as the Coddy, very soon after he received Donald Campbell's letter pleading for help in saving the piano, was to serve it up to the great and the good of the land. Air Chief Marshal Sir William Mitchell, the wartime inspector-general of the RAF, was one of the first to taste the fruits of the long row of bottles which lined the shelves of Mackenzie's library. He was on a visit to Barra to approve the site of a radio location station and he took the prof-fered dram gratefully and with reverence.

Another visitor to the Traigh Mhor was less enthusiastic. Tom Johnston, the Scottish Secretary of State who had first sent the whisky to the holds of the *Politician,* visited Mackenzie shortly afterwards. The two talked long and hard about the future of Prestwick Airport and eventually Mackenzie offered his distinguished guest a drink.

"You know I don't drink alcohol," he said severely.

"Well, you must have something to keep you going on your drive back to Castlebay through the gale."

"I'll drink half a glass of sherry."

"I'm sorry you won't sample some of our whisky. After all, you're the man we have to thank for giving us whisky galore. I'm going to write a book one day with that title. 'Galore' is a Gaelic word meaning 'plenty'."

Tom Johnston looked at the bottles of whisky round the top of the bookshelves, and then quickly swallowed that half glass of sherry as if it were firewater.

Over in South Uist, Mackenzie's namesake and fellow captain of the Home Guard, Finlay Mackenzie, was restocking the depleted supplies of his Lochboisdale Hotel with goods from the *Politician,* and using it to further the war effort. Following an exercise in the southern isles which featured some of the commandos who were then training in the West Highlands for, among other things, their tragically ill-fated raid on Dieppe, Mackenzie's Home Guard Unit was congratulated on their part in a mock "resistance" and the hotelier was invited aboard the visiting commandos' boarding steamer to dine with the officers. He took over a plentiful supply of "Polly". Halfway through his meal he heard the anchor being carefully weighed. The ship put out from Loch Boisdale into the Minch and steamed up and down off South Uist until dawn, when the officers returned Finlay Mackenzie to his native soil and at the same time collected the commandos they had left behind in South Uist, both parties being in a state of graceful good cheer.

Duncan MacInnes of Eriskay was aboard the *Politician* one day when, wandering up to the accommodation area,

> I suddenly felt strangely alone ... Looking out I saw our small boat well away from the ship with one of the men waving me to get out of sight. At first I couldn't understand why, but I soon discovered the reason.
>
> There was a naval trawler anchored off the *Polly*'s stern with a party of ratings coming on board. I streaked along that deck like lightning and hid in one of the lifeboats. Hearing their voices coming closer I plucked up courage and looked out.
>
> To my surprise they were busy looting like the rest of us and to my silent indignation they took three new oilskins belonging to my friends. We later surmised that they'd come to sink a mine blown inshore by the fierce wind. Once they'd gone I was taken off the ship and we made for home with an empty boat – the bold Navy boys had taken all our whisky.

It was not just oil-stained crofter/fishermen and their friends and families who drunk the *Politician*'s cargo that high and happy spring of 1941. They were simply the people who retrieved it. And sooner rather than later some of the whisky seeped north, to that band of labourers at the new Benbecula aero-drome, many of them the hapless unconscriptables of the main-land who had been shipped on mail-boats to work out the war in a foreign place which they dubbed "Benbeculiar", paid good wages and equipped with a formidable thirst. These guest work-ers were not well thought of by the professional classes of the islands.

"Ghastly figures," said Compton Mackenzie, who tried to persuade Whitehall to give the work that they were doing to Italian (Catholic) prisoners-of-war. "Ghastly figures who when they couldn't get whisky drank petrol, some of them, and turned blue in the face."

Donald MacAulay of the Creagorry Hotel must have thought that he had been given the monopoly to quench that thirst with something more wholesome than vehicle fuel when the licence for his public house premises at Balivanich was finally approved in April. The goods which Mr MacAulay proposed to sell would, of course, have been subject to a full payment of duty. A bottle of Mr MacAulay's whisky, for instance, would have cost roughly 16 shillings across the counter, of which 11s 4d was tax. But the alcohol which these "ghastly figures" had been buying for as little as two pounds a crate, and consuming in heroic quantities, for some weeks before Mr MacAulay had the chance to install a single beer pump, had never subscribed a penny to the Revenue.

It was a satisfactory arrangement for the people of Uist and also, no doubt, for the lowland labourers in "Benbeculiar". But it was not an arrangement designed to enchant the officials of His Majesty's Customs and Excise. The longest happy hour in the history of the Hebrides was about to be brought to a cheerless, bruising end.

FIVE

Men at Work

*These people, some of them was pretty scared, which was natural
to them, but there was some that had been away and all round
the world and they didn't think so much of it . . . It wasn't nice
at all to send these good-living honest people to prison for saving
a few bottles of whisky or whatever they might save to do some
use at the time when everything was as scarce.*
— Uist man

At the time of the grounding of the *Politician* Charles McColl
was 52 years old and had been the local officer of the Customs
and Excise for the southern isles, based at Lochboisdale, for a
number of years.

He came from the inner Hebridean island of Mull and was
therefore a Gaelic speaker – an attribute which he shared with
the people of the Uists and Barra – and a Protestant, an attribute
which he did not. A small, wiry, grey man – "grey in every way"
– Charles McColl had led, up until 1941, a peaceful life in
South Uist. He was fond of fishing with rod and line, a hobby
which the numerous fertile inland lochs of Uist easily gratified,
and of an occasional dram in good company. He had married a
South Uist woman and settled contentedly in his new island. He
was active in the small local Church of Scotland congregation
and secretary of the South Uist Mod committee, which

organised the island's annual Gaelic festival. In all of his duties, whether salaried or inspired by civic responsibility, he was thorough, tidy and methodical, keeping impeccable minutes of meetings in a neat and careful hand, writing letters and routine log-book entries in a practised and precise English. He suffered great pain, occasionally, from duodenal ulcers. McColl was, in fact, different from the main stream of professional appointees to the southern isles simply by being halfway local. He was at least an islander and a Gaelic speaker. Historically such jobs as his had been the province of Englishmen and lowland Scots anxious for a brief, interesting fling in the Highlands. "He was liked well enough, Charlie McColl," you will be told in South Uist. "He just blotted his copybook a bit on the *Politician* affair, and that took some forgiving."

As the Lochboisdale customs officer Charles McColl was directly answerable to the area's surveyor of His Majesty's Customs and Excise, who was based in Portree, the capital of the island of Skye. In 1941 that position was held by a bluff man from the north of England named Ivan Gledhill. A hearty soul outside business hours, Gledhill shared with McColl a fondness for the strict code of the Excise service. Even in wartime – *particularly* in wartime – he was determined that full and correct legislation should be applied to the lonely, winding inshore lochs and scattered islands of his new charge. As the months passed in 1941 this determination would develop into an obsession so strong that in his later life, in retirement near Lancaster in northern England, Ivan Gledhill appeared to be reluctant to admit the extent and ferocity of his involvement in the affair of the SS *Politician,* and would suggest that McColl was almost entirely responsible – "If they did wrong he [McColl] had no sympathy for them," Gledhill mused to visitors, "he'd just go right ahead."

It is difficult to judge exactly which man spurred on the other, although the correspondence of the time suggests that Gledhill, inspired initially by McColl's indignation at what was happening in the Sound of Eriskay, pursued the matter further and with more vindictiveness. But the story will tell itself, and one thing at least is sure: although Gledhill and McColl were themselves accountable to the Collector of Customs and Excise in Inverness and ultimately to the Star Chamber of the Excise Commissioners, a grand and powerful body in London, these last two bodies were not responsible for waging the bitter and one-sided sea war that raged in the southern isles throughout 1941. Gledhill and McColl did that, almost all by themselves.

Charles McColl fired his first shots as early as Saturday, 15 March. Commander Kay and his men had finished their salvage contract and departed for Glasgow three days earlier. McColl assumed, correctly, that some members of the local citizenry may have been poised to take advantage of this sudden absence of naval vessels in the Sound of Eriskay. He also assumed, equally correctly, that those men may not have been dissuaded from exploring the *Politician* by the imprimatur of the Customs Service which he had stamped forbiddingly on the hatch of Hold Number Five.

McColl dragooned from an Eriskay man a flat-bottomed, motorised boat, one of the few in the southern isles, called the *St Joseph,* and enlisted the support of the local police constable, a man from the mainland named Donald Mackenzie who, in the months that followed was – in common with others in the police force – to show an increased reluctance to fight the good Excise fight. They set off from the small natural bay at Ludag in South Uist into the Sound of Eriskay.

His first mission against the unsuspecting sailing boats of the islands was pitifully easy. No sooner had he set out, McColl reported three days later to his superiors, than

I noticed a sailing-boat, deeply laden, under sail and being rowed, proceeding in a westerly direction and apparently coming from the *Politician,* and I asked the boatman to follow this boat ... When the sailing-boat was about 25 yards away I asked them to come alongside as I wished to see what they had on board. They obeyed and I could see some cases of spirits in their cargo ... altogether twenty cases were taken from this sailing-boat.

Eight men, all from South Uist, unwittingly turned themselves over to Charles McColl from that boat. All but two of them would later serve prison sentences in Inverness Jail. McColl noticed in their small vessel "a considerable quantity of other goods pilfered from the *Politician*'s cargo", but he was, on this occasion, unable to pay further attention. Another boat appeared on the horizon, and once PC Mackenzie had finished booking and charging the men the *St Joseph* was off, once more, in hot pursuit. This second boat contained 35 cases of spirits and five men from Garrynamonie, South Uist. One of them was Donald Hector McNeil. He remembered later:

We had just come in from the *Politician* to Ludag. We were all for throwing the cases overboard – we saw the "big launch", that's what we called her, it belonged to someone in Eriskay – and we knew that the Gauger and the policeman were on board. She was alongside another boat which was further out.

We recognised her and so we said to the old fellow who was with us, "We'll throw the cases overboard and we'll pick them up again when the tide goes out."

"Och, no, you won't get them again," he said, "and anyway, no boat will get in here after us."

Right enough, we were scraping the bottom as we went into Ludag. But the big launch came in, she had a flat bottom, and the Gauger and the policeman with her. They came alongside and all we could do was to manhandle the cases into her. Throw them into her, one by one. There was other stuff in her as well, planks and everything. We claimed we got these on the tide but they took them as well and produced them at the court house when we went down there. I think one was a bit of a staircase. They took everything that was in the boat.

McColl's day was not yet done. Leaving PC Mackenzie with his seizure and his captives he set off to walk the three shoreline miles between the landing stage at Ludag and the nearest inn, at Pollochar, apparently with the intention of telephoning Finlay Mackenzie at the Lochboisdale Hotel – the same Finlay Mackenzie who was himself liberally dispensing the undutied liquor – to mobilise the Home Guard into bringing down a truck. About 100 yards from Pollochar, "I found a third boat had landed there seven further cases of spirits. I took possession of these cases and put them into safe custody." McColl also took the names of the five men from Smerclate and North Boisdale, South Uist, who had manned this third boat. They were later charged but all five were found not guilty or case not proven on a fortunate technicality. McColl alone had apprehended them. There was no police officer present, and no other witness.

Charles McColl savoured his work on that fine Saturday afternoon. On the previous Monday Ivan Gledhill and he had boarded the *Politician* and put the seal of the Customs and Excise on the hatch of Number Five Hold. He took the breaking of that seal very badly. Having deposited all of the recovered spirits in Lochboisdale Police Station, leaving them in the reluctant stewardship of PC Mackenzie, he commended Mackenzie's assistance to his superiors and suggested that the Chief Constable of Inverness-shire be notified of the fine young man working for him in the southern isles.

Then, Charles McColl came to his point. He told London:

It is a notorious fact that only a very small percentage of salved wreck goods is reported in the limits of this station and salutary penalties should be called for if and when proceedings are instituted in these cases of deliberate and organised theft; and it is further respectfully suggested that the conduct of these cases should not be left in the hands of the Procurator-Fiscal of Lochmaddy if it is desired that proper presentation of the cases be made, and that the real gravity of the position from a revenue point of view, as from others, be made properly clear.

In other words Charles McColl desired that the men he had apprehended be charged, not under the common law of theft, but under the far more punitive Customs and Excise Act. He wanted them not to be treated as pilferers, but as full-blooded looters of His Majesty's Treasury: a charge which, in wartime, would be tantamount to treason.

McColl had been deeply dissatisfied with many aspects of Commander Kay's salvage operation. Not only did the *Ranger's* haste in loading material aboard seem to him, at the time, to prevent an accurate tallying of all goods removed but he had been annoyed by Kay's refusal to mount a 24-hour guard on the whisky which he had no intention of removing, and frustrated by the fact that, as he wrote later, "it was impossible to obtain local men to maintain a shore watch". Above all, he was convinced that the Revenue was being robbed, under his very

eyes, of enormous sums of money. Of the whisky saved from the
Politician, he was to comment: "There is little doubt that practically all this has gone into consumption, largely by sale amongst
aerodrome construction gangs and partly by being forwarded to
mainland acquaintances of islanders."

McColl was in no doubt, in that March of 1941, that only
one course of action would now preserve the undutied whisky:
the remorseless hunting of offenders and the dealing out, in
high courts of law, of sentences so severe that they would echo
the length and breadth of the Scottish Gaidhealtachd. McColl
knew his islanders. He followed his urgings upon London to
prosecute to the hilt with a letter to Ivan Gledhill in Portree,
suggesting that Gledhill emphasise his advice. The jovial
Englishman did so, echoing McColl by telling his superiors that
"the feared wholesale looting and wrecking has taken place and
only extremely salutary measures will prevent an occurrence at
the next opportunity".

Gledhill and McColl had no sooner braced themselves to
fight a long and lonely legal battle when word arrived in
Lochboisdale and Portree that reinforcements from the south
were under way. Commander Kay's salvage operation had not, it
transpired, closed the book on the *Politician* so far as the authorities were concerned. Kay's Admiralty-commissioned salvage
team had not only no brief to recover whisky, they also had no
interest in scrap metal. Once they had done their job the file had
been routinely handed over to the British Iron and Steel
Corporation (Salvage) Ltd who were preparing to examine the
wreck. They would double-check Commander Kay's estimation
that the *Politician* could not be refloated. If the ship could not
be recovered in one piece they would explore the possibility of
towing away at least some part of the superstructure – it was not
unknown, in those stringent days, for two or more spoiled ships

to be grafted together to create one seaworthy vessel. And at the very least they would see if it was financially feasible to gather enough metal from the *Politician* to be shipped to Clydeside and recycled through the steelworks. The BISC (Salvage) recognised an added attraction to setting up shop in the Sound of Eriskay. Just a few hundred yards from the *Politician* lay the remains of the SS *Thala,* loaded to the gunwales with iron ore. They decided to subcontract the Job to Messrs Arnott Young Ltd of Dalmuir, near Glasgow, who had a site agent, one Percy Holden, in Lochboisdale. In wartime the BISC were obliged to collaborate with the Ministry of Supply and early in April Captain Edward Lauretson arrived in the Sound of Eriskay with his salvage vessel, the *Assistance*. Lauretson boarded the *Politician* in the eager company of Charles McColl, pronounced himself optimistic, and a week later, on 9 April, the two men went out to her again, this time in the company of Percy Holden. Holden was also impressed by the condition of the ship. McColl was not. Following this visit he wrote to Ivan Gledhill in a mood of black despair.

> You wouldn't recognise the ship now. Everything that could be taken away was taken and the rest smashed. Cases of wireless sets were opened and the sets deliberately broken to pieces.
>
> I should imagine that 300 cases have gone out of her. That, I believe, is a conservative estimate. The only thing I do hope is, even that we can't say we have the "wreckers" among the looters, that those who do go before the sheriff will be dealt with mercilessly.
>
> Tomorrow I'm going out again and after that the *Assistance* [salvage steamer] goes to Tiree to load scrap, goes to Glasgow to pick up salvage material in the shape of pumps etc., and

then gets on with the job. It seems as though the *Politician* is coming off – at least Holden and Lauretson are very optimistic about it.

I'm hoping to devote Friday and a few successive days to searching – then give it a rest, to resume after an interval when things quieten down.

McColl's assertions of random vandalism on the decks and in the holds of the *Politician* were to be repeated many times over the next few months as he and Ivan Gledhill strove to bolster their case against the island men who had flocked in small boats to the wreck. There is no doubt that many had been reckless in their treatment of the abandoned ship and that some revelry had taken place in her saloon, officers' mess and smoke room. It is true also that it is quite impossible to haul hundreds of bottles of whisky out of a dark and treacherous pit filled with oil and sea-water, using bolls of linen to hoist the prize on to a tilting deck, without some despoilment taking place. Furthermore, it is true that an unspecified amount of damage to her cargo was caused when the *Politician* first ran aground and that as the crates of whisky sat week after week immersed in salt water the wooden beams which packed them tightly together expanded. They could not then be easily removed by anybody, "looter" or salvage worker. Wood and glass was splintered and smashed, but hardly wilfully, by the conscientious diggers in Hold Number Five.

But McColl was right about the optimistic views of Percy Holden and Edward Lauretson. They had indeed decided that, while what was left of the *Thala* was good only for rough scrap, the *Politician* might, after all, be refloated.

Charles McColl, after the bitter humiliation of showing his visitors around the broken spars and shattered glass and sodden linen ropes of Hold Number Five and the evidence of lively parties over the delicate German piano in the dining saloon, was more determined than ever that the ship which they refloated would be in possession of a cargo which might no longer be quite intact, but would at least reflect in a favourable light the energy and commitment of the Customs service of the north-west coast of Scotland.

He told Ivan Gledhill that he was going "searching". This was rough code. Translated, it meant that he was intensifying a wrathful campaign to send men from South Uist and Eriskay to prison for as long as possible. All miscreants carried equal liabil-ity in the pages of the statute book and in the eyes of Charles McColl. He had no sooner posted his bitter notice of intent to Ivan Gledhill than he succeeded in nailing a man who was at home on leave after his merchant ship had been torpedoed in the English Channel and another whose recent escape from the hands of the German Army in occupied France had been the stuff of wartime legend. These are the courses which duty takes.

The morning of 12 April 1941 dawned clear and fine. The Sound of Eriskay was at its translucent best, extreme spring tides uncovered at the lowest ebb yards of rack and shellfish-coated rock and glittering stretches of bright white sand. The tides were also important to those who breached the high plate-metal walls of the grounded *Politician*. Charles McColl and PC Donald Mackenzie boarded the *St Joseph* once again, and puttered out onto the azure sea.

They had not travelled far before a sailing-boat hove into view, leaving the *Politician* in some haste and making for Eriskay. Upon reaching the shore, McColl found the sailing-boat moored and anchored, and close to it three men in a rowing-boat, lifting the line of a lobster creel.

"We went alongside this boat," the Gauger recorded, "and found one man covered in crude oil, a second wearing an oilskin badly smeared with oil, the third being as far as could be seen free from oil contamination." This was damning evidence. As McColl explained to his superiors:

> The cargo of the *Politician* included roughly 21,000 cases and cartons of whisky, all stowed in Number Five Hold, and this hold, which is tidal, i.e. the water in the hold rises and falls with the tide, has a coating of three to four inches of crude oil.
>
> The procedure of the looters would seem to be that one man goes into the hold, gets the cases and fixes a rope around each to be hauled on to the next deck by number two. The third man remains in the boat alongside the ship, and number one and number two lower the cases to him there. This would account for one man being covered in oil, one less so, and the third being completely free of oil.

McColl and Mackenzie found the rowing-boat to be empty, and turned their attention to the sailing smack. In this they found 17 cases of whisky and a bag containing ten bottles – the remains of a sodden and broken cardboard carton. They returned to the rowing-boat, where the three men denied having been aboard the wreck. McColl expostulated that the state of their clothing indicated otherwise, and one man replied: "Very likely." Under further questioning they then informed McColl that a second boat had been at the ship that day and was last seen heading north to Loch Boisdale. If the customs launch set off promptly, it might catch up. McColl, however, was accepting no King's Evidence. "It is hardly likely," he deliberated later, "that he would be able to give this information, and especially specify the township from which the men were, if both crews had not been on board the *Politician* together."

The *St Joseph* gave chase, and after two and a half hours it overhauled the second boat just as it was approaching the shadowy safety of the entrance to Loch Boisdale. Catching it was no difficult feat – "it contained about as much whisky in cases and cartons as it could with safety accommodate".

The wind was getting up and McColl insouciantly asked the four men aboard if they would care for a tow into Loch Boisdale. They replied, no, they were not going there. McColl kept the *St Joseph* alongside, however, and eventually the Uistmen gave in and allowed themselves to be towed to the shore where McColl and Mackenzie uncovered the prodigious haul of 14 cases and 225 loose bottles of whisky, and two bicycle mudguards.

It would appear to be reasonable to suggest, McColl later told London:

> that no one member of the crew could be expected to consume eight cases of whisky, which is roughly what each man's share would be, and that the ultimate disposal of the spirits would be by sale ... (they) say they went out to "salvage" the whisky and bring it to Lochboisdale ... When charged by the constable one man replied: "I went out more or less to see the boat. We were bringing the whisky to Lochboisdale."

> It is estimated that at least 500–1,000 cases have been looted from the ship, which being stranded eight miles from Lochboisdale is extremely difficult to keep under observation, especially as no motor boat is available at Lochboisdale. It is believed that a considerable quantity of the looted spirits is buried in and around the shores of Eriskay and South Uist,

and once the cargo is lifted by the salvors, who hope to commence operations early next week, and whose first work will be to remove the cargo, a systematic search as far as that is possible will be made with the object of securing some of the goods.

The charging of the four-man crew of this second boat on that day in April puts the activity of the Customs and Excise into a certain perspective. Two of the "looters" were brothers, James and Neil Campbell. Being based in Lochboisdale, neither McColl nor Mackenzie could have been entirely unaware of the circumstances and recent history of these two men, whom McColl wished to have branded as rather worse than common criminals, men whom he and Ivan Gledhill were urging the full majesty of the law to penalise as unpatriotic swindlers of the Treasury. James Campbell was a merchant seaman, temporarily at home on leave after his ship had been attacked and sunk in the English Channel by a German U-boat. Before long he would be willingly back at sea.

His brother, Neil, had nine months earlier displayed the kind of courage and clear-eyed initiative for which medals are minted. On 9 June 1940, after fighting for almost a week in the lost battle of the Somme, Neil Campbell was ordered to make his way south for evacuation. He had not eaten for two days. On 10 June he and 8,000 others were forced to surrender at St Valery-en-Caux. He was herded with his companions into a field and then forced off on the long march to Poland.

Neil Campbell never saw Poland. After ten miles marching on that first day of captivity he and a friend regained their freedom in the late afternoon, escaping from the line by the chillingly simple expedient of opening the front door of a roadside house as they passed it, slipping inside, closing the door behind them, breaking out through a back window and hiding in the long grass until dark. At dawn on the following day they made for a wood and hid again.

On 13 June they ate for the first time in six days, a meal of raw potatoes dug out of the ground. On the morning of 17 June, seven days after their escape, seven days of criss-crossing the hazardous, chaotic countryside of northern France, they ate pickled bacon, bread, and milk taken – looted? – from villages occupied by German soldiers. It was their first meal for nine days and it strengthened their resolve to return to Britain. For four days and nights they hid in a mansion-house outside Dieppe and then approached the town and, for another four days, took the lie of the land.

On 28 June they slid past German guards into Dieppe harbour and located a suitable 24-foot sailing-boat. For almost a week they stocked the boat with food, and at midnight on 3 July they "determined on a desperate dash for the open sea and freedom". Neil Campbell later recalled:

Luckily I could handle boats since I can remember. I sorted sails, rigging and blocks and made her fit to cast off. At midnight we lifted the anchor and steered down the river to the bridge. Alas! The lock gates under the bridge were barred. We tried to open them but it was impossible. We tried to get back to the place where we were previously anchored, but the receding tide racing outwards proved too strong. We saw four other boats anchored beside the bridge and took our boat in between two of them . . .

Early the next morning two Germans came into the boat next to us and began sorting the engine, talking and laughing. Guards on the bridge walked to and fro all day. We had a shotgun and ammunition from the mansion and were not to be caught without a stiff fight for it. Evening came and the Germans went away without noticing us.

Before dark we had a peek at the bridge – a gate was open at the faraway side. Before launching on our last dash we put the engine on the boat they had so carefully sorted out of action. I pulled out all the cables and plugs and threw them into the river. At midnight we sailed out, past the bridge and out as far as the mouth of the river before being heard by the guard. He started shouting and fired a warning shot; we rowed desperately. He fired a second shot – we were about 100 yards out, getting the full force of the strong gale which was blowing. The guard apparently could not see us, although the splash of the oars could probably be seen, as the third shot blew our oars into smithereens.

We had to get the mast and the sail up. Being very heavy it wasn't easy, and machine-gun bursts from shore batteries fell like hail around us. Heavy seas washed over the deck but we got the mast and sail up and sped for home.

The following day, with the French coast still visible astern, the gale split Neil Campbell's sail clean in two. He fixed it, only to see the jib and the rigging blow apart. He climbed the mast and once again got the ketch under way.

That evening they sighted the coast of southern England and a minesweeper, the HMT *Dalmatia,* picked them up. They had crossed 52 miles of the English Channel, in a gale, in 16 hours. It had taken them 25 days from the Fall of France to reaching British soil.

"We were granted leave," remembered Campbell, "and I made at once for my home in South Uist. On landing at Lochboisdale, I could hardly speak thinking of my comrades marching wearily to Germany – the privations of their captivity.

I was glad to be back. All my privations and hunger endured were all forgotten with one glimpse of home."

Within the year Neil Campbell, once again a private in the Cameron Highlanders and home on leave from active service with the re-formed Highland Division, found himself in another boat, being threatened with incarceration by another, wholly unexpected, authority. He was, fortunately, a good-natured man.

The second salvage operation on the SS *Politician,* commissioned by the British Iron & Steel Corporation in collaboration with the Ministry of Supply, and carried out by Arnott Young, got underway when Captain Edward Lauretson and the *Assistance* returned from Tiree and Glasgow on 21 April. Although this salvage was to be chiefly concerned with attempts to refloat the vessel, with a view to taking her back to the mainland where she could possibly be patched up, or be grafted on to the torn parts of another ship, or at the worst be more efficiently converted into scrap, McColl and Gledhill persuaded the salvors to do what Commander Kay had seen no point in doing: to unload the whisky and return it to warehouses on dry land.

With some satisfaction Ivan Gledhill reported to the Customs Commissioners in London that Lauretson's salvage crews "have promised to give first attention to the clearing of Number Five Hold. The goods will be sent coastwise under sealed hatches to Glasgow. When the hold is cleared it will be possible to form some estimate of the extent of the looting." Not that Lauretson was entirely co-operative. He was obliged to inform Gledhill, to the latter's disappointment, that he and his men were not in the least bit interested in helping to reclaim goods which had already gone missing from the *Politician's* cargo. Under pressure from Gledhill, Lauretson did, however, offer an off-the-cuff estimate of the amount of damage done to the interior of the ship.

Gledhill promptly used this in a letter to London, attempting to further blacken the characters of those who dared to break the Customs' seal, to stress to his office-bound superiors the formidable enemy which confronted Charles McColl and himself, and to give further weight to his campaign for the strictest possible sentences. "Had the vessel been refloated," Ivan Gledhill wrote, "it would have required an expenditure of at least £10,000 to repair the wanton damage done to the vessel by the looters, who appear to have indulged in a perfect orgy of awful destruction in addition to looting."

None of this was the business of Edward Lauretson or of Percy Holden. A series of coasters and lighters began to arrive from Clydeside and Troon and the contents of Hold Number Five were loaded into them. At least some of it was. Donald MacDiarmid of Ardnamurchan, the most westerly point on the British mainland, recalled working on a salvage vessel when it was detailed to the Sound of Eriskay in 1941:

We were working on a boat that went aground off Cumbrae Head, when we got word to go to Lochboisdale. We hadn't a clue what was in the *Politician* until we arrived – of course it was wartime and things were more secretive. Anyway, when we arrived we went into Lochboisdale and someone there took us around to where the wreck was.

There was another boat alongside and she was supposed to let us in – we had pumps on board. Anyway, the crew must have got a hold of some whisky because they weren't capable of doing anything, far less letting us in alongside. The skipper went up to the bridge and rang the telegraph. No one answered from down below. So all he did was to let her ropes go and the current took her away. One of the crew dropped her anchor and we got in.

We were to take the whisky out of the big boat, but her fuel tanks had burst and the thick black oil filled the holds. The oil rose to the top of the water, so when the slings went down and were loaded by the divers, on the way up they had to come through this layer of oil – it was a real mess. All they did was lift the loads and throw them into our hold, and we brought the stuff into Lochboisdale. Then others would come on board and pick out the better, cleaner cases, and these were taken away to Glasgow, or somewhere in the south.

That didn't last; we were detailed to throw the rest into the sea because it was considered hardly worth while to take the stuff away, there being no duty paid on it.

There was a Lochboisdale man with me and he was working on lobster creels. One night when we were returning from the *Politician* to Lochboisdale he said, "Come out with me to lift the creels." They were near Calvay Island. Every one we lifted had half a dozen bottles in it! Most of the stuff was taken by others. There was only one Customs officer, and he couldn't be there every day.

In the months that followed, the second salvage operation succeeded in recovering the equivalent of 13,500 cases of whisky, three casks of whisky, one cask of beer and one cask of sherry. They did not empty Number Five Hold, much of its contents being considered irredeemable; they threw a lot away, as Donald MacDiarmid testifies; and the salvors and the crews of the coasting vessels had no compunction about drinking the stuff themselves, or even about bringing home quantities of it to the island families with whom they were lodged. Nobody, it was apparent, gave a fig for the sanctity of the contents of Hold Number Five of the SS *Politician*. Nobody except Charles McColl and Ivan Gledhill.

While whisky from the *Politician* was being lifted by the men who were employed to salve it, drunk by Air Chief Marshals and naval captains lucky enough to be assigned to the area, openly sold in local hotels, "pilfered" by passing sailors from Royal Naval minesweepers and thrown in quantity into the sea from Lochboisdale pier, men were being sent to jail from Lochmaddy Sheriff Court and Ivan Gledhill and Charles McColl were planning a series of punitive raids on the homes of the people of the southern isles.

SIX

Not Guilty

The customs came round. We had two cases or something like that. They took it all away. We were summoned to go down to Lochmaddy. Six weeks it was, the sentence that we got, or one month. We was very quiet and very nice people.
— Eriskay woman

The first cases to be prosecuted in the affair of the SS *Politician* were heard at the early date of 26 April at Lochmaddy Sheriff Court, a lofty Victorian granite slab which sits like a severe grandparent in the largest township in North Uist.

The defendants were from Barra. They were the first and the last men from that island to be prosecuted, despite the fact that a substantial amount of the *Polly's* cargo found its way to Northbay, Eoligarry and Castlebay. Barra and Vatersay, like the northern and inner Hebrides, were effectively beyond the reach of Charles McColl's jurisdiction; these Barra men who walked into the dock at Lochmaddy on 26 April had not been apprehended by McColl, or by PC Donald Mackenzie, or by Ivan Gledhill. They had been caught by the Barra police. Three days earlier, on 23 April, the constabulary at Northbay had been unable to avoid five men in a boat which contained two cases of whisky and some drums of oil. Four of the five men were charged and taken to Lochmaddy, where they were held in custody until their cases were rushed through. The men pled guilty to charges of theft and Sheriff-Substitute Donald fined two of them five pounds each and two of them three pounds each.

When the news reached Portree, Ivan Gledhill was dismayed. Gledhill had only just been able to inform his superiors that more than 30 men, caught as the result of the labours of Charles McColl and Donald Mackenzie, would be appearing at Lochmaddy on 13 May. The idea of them being obliged to pay only middling fines rather than suffer the obloquy of the state and a lengthy term of imprisonment filled Ivan Gledhill with horror. The constabulary and the courts were, he claimed, being less than co-operative. "No notification," he complained, "from the Barra police has been received either of the seizure or of the proceedings."

Gledhill was mainly exercised, however, by the fact that common law charges of theft were being pursued and his own recommendation that action be taken under the Customs and Excise Act was consequently ignored:

The officer's [Charles McColl's] attendance is not required [in court] and I am informed that all proceedings are under the Summary Jurisdiction Act, 1908. If so it appears probable that merely small fines will be imposed which will not have the effect of a general deterrent on the population.

In my opinion nothing but imprisonment of a few of the worst offenders is likely to produce any general respect for the law. The officer is of the opinion that hundreds of cases of whisky have been looted and that it is mainly hidden on the moors to be recovered when the opportunity offers.

He is of the opinion that sales of the looted spirit are taking place on the aerodrome constructions work at Benbecula, and that neither he nor the police will be able to

S.S. POLITICIAN

TOP AND ABOVE: A sleek, fast, and handsome vessel – the ss *London Merchant*, which was renamed the *Politician*

The naval prodigy, Captain Beaconsfield Worthington

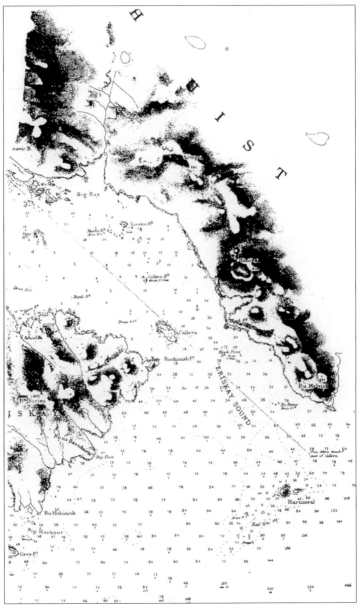

Treacherous waters – the Admiralty Sea Chart of the Sound of Eriskay

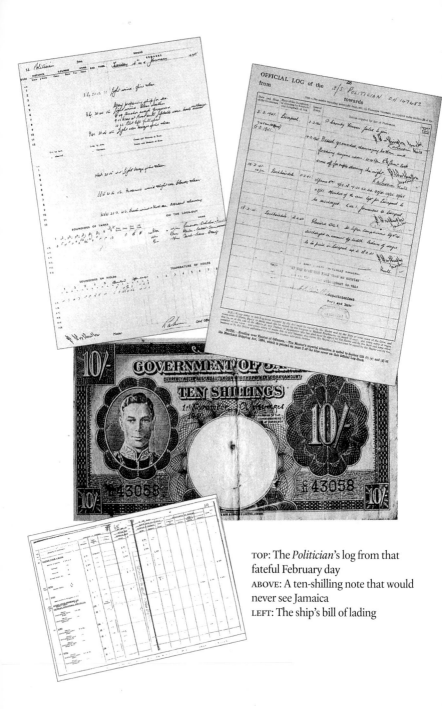

TOP: The *Politician*'s log from that
fateful February day
ABOVE: A ten-shilling note that would
never see Jamaica
LEFT: The ship's bill of lading

TOP LEFT: The *Highland News* gets an international scoop TOP RIGHT: a bottle of 'Polly' ABOVE: 'I would strongly urge that action be taken . . .' – McColl and Gledhill correspond

Compton Mackenzie above Castlebay on the island of Barra

Islanders were only mildly surprised to see film technicians laying artificial granite over unphotogenic local stones

Local croft houses were deemed inauthentic and too gloomy for interior shooting, and strange replicas appeared outside Castlebay

'The humour is a surprise to us . . . for an Englishman, it is so Gallic'

obtain any evidence. It is submitted for consideration as to whether this aspect might merit the attention of the Special Inquiry Branch . . .

This same Ivan Gledhill mused in later years: "Always in the islands they have regarded a wreck as their own property. Though I cannot approve, I can sympathise."

In 1941 his customs operation showed few signs of sympathy. They moved quickly from thrilling sea chases to the prosecution of their duties on dry land, to invading the everyday life of the quiet islands. Convinced that substantial quantities of whisky were leaving the southern isles by His Majesty's mails (some bottles were sent to friends and relatives on the mainland), McColl and Gledhill petitioned the postmaster at Lochboisdale to intercept and open any suspicious-looking parcels. He fobbed them off with a noncommittal answer and promptly, to their fury, broadcast the word locally that no more whisky should be sent by post. The Lochboisdale postmaster had no intention of meddling with the mails himself, he made clear to his friends and neighbours, but he could not speak for his colleagues in the nearest sorting office, on the mainland at Oban.

Letters to the interim Procurator-Fiscal, the Scottish public prosecutor, in Lochmaddy, John Gray, reaped little better reward for the customs men. On 28 May Gray wrote to Gledhill:

As you are aware, proceedings were instituted against the accused on charges of theft at common law, and these instructions were given before your letter of 13th inst. was received. In these circumstances crown counsel consider that it is preferable to proceed against the accused on the common law charges to theft, rather than on the statutory charges.

The increasing unwillingness of the police to co-operate in an exercise that was doing little for public relations, the refusal of the courts to elevate their common law charges, the nonchalance of the salvage men and even the apparent indifference of their own bosses in London could not dampen the ardour of the crusading customs men. They began to raid houses.

Customs officials have, in many respects, greater powers than the police force when it comes to opening the doors of private residences, and Charles McColl had begun to exercise these powers as early as 17 March when he and Donald Mackenzie made a thorough investigation of the dwelling-places of some of the men they had already collared at sea and of others who were simply prime suspects. On 17 March, two days after their first expedition on the *St Joseph,* they turned over houses in Garrynamonie. A variety of interesting goods were uncovered: washing soda, a tarpaulin, shovels and rolls of canvas and cloth; but only three bottles of whisky – hardly the evidence required to shake Whitehall.

They progressed to the house of James and Neil Campbell, who were yet to be arraigned on the high seas, and came away with:

Six cakes of soap, three erasers, two boxes of rubber bands, and two notebooks, four lavatory-basin plugs and chains, a bottle of ink, a tin-opener, a potato peeler, a roll of bandage, a thermometer, three signal rockets, a roll of lamp wick, and some bottles of disinfectant.

But no whisky.

On 22 March they paid a call on Donald Hector McNeil in Garrynamonie and found "thirteen packets of Capstan cigarettes, each pack containing ten cigarettes; two cycle mudguards . . ." But still no whisky.

On 5 May their luck changed. Being unable to commission the *St Joseph* from Eriskay in time to intercept two vessels which McColl and Mackenzie spotted leaving the *Politician,* they walked from Ludag into South Glendale in the hope of intercepting one of them. There was no road at the time between the two villages, and so:

This involved a walk over moor and bog of two and a half miles and it was questionable whether we could cover the distance before the boat got in. But a low tide prevented the boat landing near the head of Glendale Bay where we had taken up position and were concealed from view.

Shortly after our arrival at the head of the bay we saw about half a mile away figures against the sky on a headland and watched three men walk along to the side of the bay opposite to that on which we were concealed. As they approached the head of the bay we moved across to them in the gathering dark, and walking on sand as we were they were unaware of our presence until I spoke to them.

One of them was carrying a sack and I asked him what he had there. He dropped the sack but said nothing. The second man had moved off to the left and was apprehended by the police constable. I questioned the party who admitted having taken the goods in the sack – twelve bottles of sherry sack, bottled and exported by William Gilbey Ltd and identified as part of the cargo of SS *Politician* from a consignment of 60 cases of sherry appearing in the ship's manifest as shipped by Gilbeys from the stranded ship.

The "man" with the sack of sherry was, in fact, not yet a man, he was a 14-year-old boy. He was, nonetheless, charged and the details of his case were sent to the Procurator-Fiscal in Lochmaddy. This instigated a bizarre chain of events, even by the standards of the day.

The local government officer for the islands of Benbecula, South Uist and Eriskay at that time was a local man named John MacInnes. His duties were manifold. MacInnes was responsible for collecting rates, instituting welfare payments, serving on the education subcommittee – the broad panoply of state affairs in the islands was watched over by John MacInnes. And in wartime he had an extra, unrequested, task. It was his job to notify the families of the deceased that their sons, brothers and husbands had been lost in action.

When the law in Lochmaddy received details of the charging of a boy from South Glendale, barely into his teens, with theft (and possibly worse) they commissioned John MacInnes to visit his home. MacInnes recalled:

For a start he should have been at school that day. I was the clerk of the education subcommittee, and I had to write a report on the conditions and the home surroundings. The parish minister at the time was Reverend Malcolm Laing and he had to go as well, but he and I were not supposed to go together.

I said to him, "This is a lot of kerfuffle. You know as well as I do about this place, and we'll just go together." I said, "I've got to go to Eriskay and we'll get into Glendale after half low tide. You go up and pass the time with the parish priest, I'll call for you, and both of us will go to see that house." I knew the conditions before I left, but I don't think he did – he was surprised to see that it was a very nice house.

Reverend Malcolm Laing was not the only person to receive a surprise that day. The mother of the teenaged boy was unaccustomed to receiving visits from the minister and the government official, together, at the same time. She also had two other sons serving in the merchant navy. Inevitably, she assumed the worst. John MacInnes remembered:

> The woman went into hysterics. When she saw us calling, it was, Oh they've drowned, something's happened! She had real hysterics, threw herself around. I tried to pacify her. I knew her from school. I said, "We're not concerned with that at all, it's not *that* that's happened – it's this scallywag with the wine bottles, and we've got to send a report in."
>
> I said to her, "What he did was . . . well, there's nothing to it. I would have done it. Anybody would have done it." I told her that, once upon a time I would have done it too . . .

The cases against 35 men and one boy from South Uist and Eriskay were heard for the first time in Lochmaddy Sheriff Court on 13 May 1941. They were charged with theft by the interim Procurator-Fiscal, John Gray. Four of them entered a plea of guilty, and they were fined four pounds, three pounds and, in two cases, two pounds. The remaining 32 pled not guilty. Their cases were adjourned by Sheriff-Substitute Donald until the next court session, which was due to start on 10 June. Charles McColl and Ivan Gledhill determined not to be idle in the intervening weeks.

Early in June the two customs men called in reinforcements. They enlisted the help of the islands' other customs officer, Edward Bootham White, who was based at Tarbert in the island of Harris, and they persuaded William Fraser, the Chief Constable of Inverness-shire, to send over to the southern isles two police sergeants from the mainland, G. N. Richards and Arnold Stephens. The introduction of these officers to the campaign was only partly intended to strengthen Gledhill's squad; Donald Mackenzie, along with his colleagues in Barra, was becoming increasingly concerned about his role in the events and about his ability to function within such a tight-knit community once the storm had passed. Although the recaptured crates and bottles continued to pile up around his desk in the cramped Lochboisdale police office, Mackenzie himself slowly slipped back from the front line.

McColl, Bootham White, Richards and Stephens raided houses and crofts in Eriskay and South Uist on 6 and 7 June, three days before the cases of the 32 men were due to be heard at Lochmaddy. Much has been made since of these raids: of the destroying of peat stacks, forced entry into houses, disturbing of innocent old people, and there is no doubt that for a brief period some small communities were subjected to an unnecessary, disproportionately harsh harassment. But the sadder truth, for Ivan Gledhill and Charles McColl, is that the raids of early June, like the raids of March, were spectacularly unsuccessful. Gledhill might have complained to his bosses that the fault for such failure was that of the police – "The ineffective result," he wrote, "was due to the fact that on the first day the local inspector of police refused to continue the search after lunchtime. It is now certain that on the same night there was a general conveyance of spirits to the moors and hills by the looters and the matter of finding them is now one of extreme difficulty" – but, in truth, he must at this stage have heard the beating of the wings of defeat.

Bootham White and Sergeants Richards and Stephens submitted their own account of their activities on South Uist and Eriskay on 6 and 7 June. It made quite different reading from the panicked pleas of McColl and Gledhill. After a sorry day in Eriskay, when they found a couple of cases of whisky, "some lengths of hose and two buckets", the officers returned to the island on the following morning. They stressed:

> Spirits were found but there was abundant evidence that goods had been hurriedly unearthed, and attempts to trace the place to which the goods had been removed suggested that they had been taken by boats either to a more remote part of the coast or to the small islands in the vicinity. The sites where goods had been removed were frequently in the middle of growing crops.

After the disappointment of Eriskay, McColl insisted on taking his accomplices to that hotbed of piracy, South Glendale in South Uist. There, he was sure, rich pickings would be had. They searched seven crofts in South Glendale – virtually the full extent of the village. The officers reported:

> Nothing was found in the crofts, but a sack was found in the peat containing a ship's compass, three brushes, one fire bucket, three plates, five salad dishes and four rubber pedals. No search could be made on Monday 9th June owing to stormy weather. All the goods found were removed under police supervision to Lochboisdale police station.

Gledhill kept a brave face. "I am satisfied that there are considerable quantities of other cargo, including spirits and equipment, yet undiscovered," he wrote in a covering letter, a minority report; but the first and the last full-scale "joint operation" between the police and customs to reclaim the cargo of the *Politician* from the crofts of the southern isles was ignominiously called off. Charles McColl and Ivan Gledhill, who had been begging for support from the other services for months, felt badly let down. PC Donald Mackenzie was left fuming beneath a cornucopia of kitchenware, fire-fighting apparatus, bicycle accessories and untouchable bottles of whisky.

Almost all of the 32 men from South Uist and Eriskay appeared in person at Lochmaddy Sheriff Court between 10 June and 13 June to answer charges of theft. They had entered pleas of not guilty, not out of any capricious attempt to escape punishment – the cases previously heard had clearly indicated that pleas of guilty were likely to elicit the response of a moderate fine – but because, unadvised as they were by any legal counsel, they genuinely believed that whatever wrongs they may have committed on God's earth, theft from the SS *Politician* was not among them.

This time Charles McColl was called and allowed to give evidence. He testified that the greater part of the men's offences was that of stealing from a ship which was still seaworthy. A rumble went around the courtroom as McColl informed Sheriff-Substitute Donald that the *Politician* would, in fact, be floated again. Her sojourn in the Sound of Eriskay was no more than a brief, regrettable interruption of normal trading duties.

Sheriff-Substitute Donald pondered and finally agreed with McColl. Only one of the men was found not guilty. Nine others were dismissed from the court with their cases not proven, that halfway house in Scottish law which manages to drop a prosecution without completely clearing the name of the defendant. In the instance of the teenaged boy from South Glendale the prosecution deserted its case following John MacInnes's and Reverend Laing's report. His elder brother, the man who had "moved off to the left" on that shadowy evening in May, took the brunt. He was sentenced to 20 days' imprisonment. And so were 18 others, sentenced to be taken down to Inverness Prison, 200 miles away by sea and land, for a variety of terms. With the exception of a couple who escaped with small fines, all of the men found guilty – 19 of them – were given terms of imprisonment which varied from 20 days to two months.

Donald Hector McNeil received a sentence of four weeks. James Campbell was sent down for six and thereby found his leave from the merchant navy considerably extended. James's brother Neil, who had been caught in the same boat at the same time with the same whisky, found his case not proven and was able to walk free back to his regiment. The three men from Eriskay, whom McColl and Mackenzie had found covered in oil and innocently hauling lobster pots next to their incriminating sailing smack, got 30 days each.

The hearings were not without their lighter moments. Roderick Campbell was asked at one stage if, in support of his not guilty plea, he was actually denying that he had been aboard the *Politician*.

"No," he replied.

"Then you have been aboard her?" pressed procurator-fiscal John Gray.

"Oh yes."

"And when would that have been?"

"I can't remember exactly. Nineteen-twenty-something, I think. I was in Vancouver, and so was she, and I went aboard to visit my brother who was a seaman on her at the time."

Roderick Campbell's case was found not proven, as was that of his brother Angus John and that of the old man from Garrynamonie whom McColl, having caught him red-handed, reported to headquarters as being "82 years old, *and in receipt of an old age pension*".

But the bulk of the men had to grit their teeth and prepare for the journey to Inverness. All of the pressure which had been put on the legal authorities by Charles McColl and Ivan Gledhill, all of the wild allegations about the vandalism and black-market-eering, all of the cautions about the anarchy which lay dormant in the southern isles and which would only be lulled back to sleep by exemplary prison sentences; all of this, and the startling news that the *Politician* and her cargo were waiting to be refloated (which was received with surprise and considerable scepticism by the accused men) had, it seemed, paid off.

Extraordinarily, Ivan Gledhill and Charles McColl were not satisfied.

It is possible that when the sentences were handed out the customs men were still smarting from their humiliating searches of Eriskay and South Uist. It is certain that, having won some guilty verdicts in the face of what they perceived as lack of co-operation from the court officials at Lochmaddy, McColl and Gledhill found themselves reflecting frustratedly on the kind of sentences that might have been passed down if they had won their campaign to get the men prosecuted under the Customs Act rather than on the common law charge of theft.

Ivan Gledhill was not in the court at Lochmaddy that second week in June but when he heard of the sentences he wrote to Procurator-Fiscal Gray to protest about their leniency. He then wrote to his commissioners in London to tell them that he had written to the Procurator-Fiscal, adding:

In my opinion these few small sentences are quite inadequate to act as a general deterrent to the population of these islands, who in my opinion will probably seize their next opportunity to further looting and damage.

A few days later Gledhill received a full account of the proceedings at Lochmaddy Sheriff Court and he decided to write again to London, this time reasserting his belief that the paltry charge of theft was insufficient for offences of this magnitude. "I am informed that the maximum sentence under this charge," he said, "is three months, and this appears totally inadequate to affect the local outlook on the wreck or to prevent a recurrence of similar practice at the next opportunity."

Ivan Gledhill's conviction that the islanders were quite insensitive to such trivialities as having to spend two months in Inverness Prison was not well founded. The men accepted the turn that events had taken with stoicism and humour – there was no other way – but they were offended and made angry by the perversion of natural justice, by the stain unreasonably put upon their characters and not least by the fact that each one of them, members of possibly the most peaceable and law-abiding community in Britain, now had a criminal record. "It wasn't nice at all . . ."

On the evening of 10 June, when news of the first prison sentences seeped down to Lochboisdale, the affair of the *Politician* appeared briefly to be getting out of control. Charles McColl kept his car in a shared garage in Lochboisdale and that evening a hole was made in the roof of the garage, petrol poured through it and a lighted match sent in after that. McColl's car was only slightly damaged but another was totally destroyed. "It is practically certain," reported Ivan Gledhill, "that this was done by persons concerned in the *Politician* looting." It was more likely to have been done by persons concerned that their friends or relatives had just been sent to jail. But sense prevailed, privately and quietly, articulated no doubt by priests and village elders. No further incidents of the kind took place, although

Gledhill requested of London that "he [McColl] be not concerned in any further general search".

It being wartime, the convicted men were at least spared the great ignominy which is traditionally inflicted by the Highland press upon their readers who are unfortunate enough to appear in courts of law. In peacetime the merest shoplifter may be given headline treatment by many a Highland newspaper: the whisky looters from the southern isles could have expected little mercy. In fact, their activities were blacked out as efficiently as an Inverness street lamp.

When the *Politician* first ran aground the rumour spread that the Nazi propagandist William Joyce – better known as "Lord Haw-Haw" – had broadcast that she had been lost with all hands. At least Joyce mentioned the ship. The British media, with one exception, carefully avoided her until the war was safely over.

That one exception was a Highland newspaper, the *Highland News*. In common with many rural weeklies, then and now, the *Highland News* had a network of busy local correspondents, unpaid contributors who pledged to keep the paper up to date on such matters as the fate of the harvest and the satisfactory matching of young couples. The *Highland News* correspondent in North Uist took his or her duties a little further. He or she actually attended the sessions of Lochmaddy Sheriff Court.

Thus it was that on 24 May the *Highland News* mentioned that a number of men had appeared in Lochmaddy "to answer to a charge of theft of whisky and other articles. Several pled guilty and charges were imposed, while the remaining cases . . . were adjourned for proof."

And so it was that on 21 June the *Highland News* became the first newspaper in the world to win a headline story from the SS *Politician*. Not that the ship was mentioned, nor any of the relevant details – this was wartime, and stories of British citizens removing articles from stranded British merchantmen were sensitive indeed. But under the tempting lead "THEFTS OF WHISKY" the *Highland News*'s North Uist correspondent broke a story which could, in happier days, have made a journalist famous. The news item ran:

> At a recent sitting of the Sheriff Court at which Sheriff-Substitute D.A. Donald, Portree, presided, local men from various parts of South Uist, including the Island of Eriskay, were sentenced to terms of imprisonment ranging from one to two months, while a number were fined in sums ranging from £3 to £10. All were charged with theft and the property stolen included cases of whisky and other goods. Pleas of not guilty were tendered. Mr John Gray, interim procurator-fiscal, conducted the prosecution. The trials lasted from Tuesday to Friday and created a good deal of local interest.

Below this paragraph we learn of other sentences handed out by Mr Donald at that session of the Sheriff Court. A Glasgow labourer, employed at Benbecula, answered a charge of "assaulting a fellow workman by striking him on the head with a bottle to the effusion of blood". A soldier home on leave had committed a breach of the peace at Creagorry Hotel and "assaulted two constables while being forcibly ejected from the premises". Neither of these two men were as harshly sentenced as those from Eriskay and South Uist, all with previously clean records, who found themselves in Inverness Prison for saving whisky from the sea.

But Ivan Gledhill's writ was not yet run. Each time his men had made a seizure they had either confiscated the boat or painted upon it an arrow, with a view to identifying it for later confiscation. By June Charles McColl had a small flotilla of these hardy old island cobles on his hands and Gledhill was looking to increase the fleet. Letters came in from local men, anxious that the lobster season was passing them by, requesting the return of their vessels. The father of James and Neil Campbell, now that one of his sons was tucked away in prison and the other returned to the desert war, felt that possibly he might get his boat back. Angus Campbell wrote to Gledhill on 27 June:

I wish to explain that the boat was used on the occasion on which it was intercepted without my knowledge, my consent, and against my strict instructions that it was not to be taken. I regard it as a hardship that I should be punished for an offence in which I had no part.

The boat is 15 foot long and is 43 years of age, and except for myself and occasional fishing has no value. I would point out that being unpainted and unattended during the hot summer weather a boat of her age will split open altogether and become quite useless, especially as she is drawn out of the water. I respectfully ask that the boat be handed back to me under the circumstances, but if you do not see your way to doing so, to prevent her rotting on the ground and becoming derelict for all time I am willing to pay the sum of two pounds.

Another man wrote:

My boat had been used by some boys to take stuff out of the *Politician,* a steamer that went on the rocks in Eriskay Sound about the ninth of February. As the salvage boats left and no watchman or any other sign was put up, being considered a total wreck the boys decided to go up and take my boat with them without my knowledge or consent For taking my boat for the purpose the Excise authorities seized her and now I am unable to do my fishing as is my usual occupation.

As the boat belongs to me I consider it a very unfair treatment to take her from me as I depended on the boat for my living. The lobster fishing starts early in June and now I am unable to begin fishing lobsters when my boat is taken from me. If a watch had been put aboard the *Politician* when she went on the rocks there would have been no trouble as some men offered to take the job. If you will see your way in releasing my boat to let me earn my living I shall appreciate the fact and await your immediate reply.

It was not only the fishing that suffered through Gledhill and McColl's hijacking of the small boats of South Uist. A man wrote to Gledhill in June:

On Thursday 15th last, an Excise officer called at my home and told me that I was not to use my boat . . . as it has now become the property of the Crown. He put a ticket on the boat to this effect. I complained to this officer that I would require the boat to attend to my stock which are on an island off the coast of South Uist and cannot be reached by any other means. While he was quite sympathetic on this matter he told me he could not release the boat, but he advised me to write to Portree.

I now appeal that the boat be released so that I can attend to my stock. I made every endeavour to secure another boat but without success. I have 200 sheep and lambs on this island and it is possible that some of them are dying with the want of attention, and in times like this when everybody is doing his best in the national interest it is a pity to see the stock going to waste. Under these circumstances I trust you will see your way of letting me have the use of my boat.

But far from considering the release of the sequestrated boats, Ivan Gledhill became increasingly convinced that their seizure represented the neatest solution to his problem. Let down by the police force and betrayed by the milksop courts of law, he could at least exercise his own local powers and, in doing so, both punish the local community and keep them off the Sound of Eriskay. He told McColl to hold on to what he had and went in search of further prey.

He had been unable to locate and immobilise two vessels which were of particular importance. One was the sailing smack from Eriskay which McColl and Mackenzie had searched on one of their earlier outings. On 25 June, while the three men caught on that boat were still in jail, Gledhill visited the southern isles and travelled, with McColl, to Eriskay. They had the registration number of the boat – CY 408 – and they had its recent history. But they could find it nowhere. They made an extensive search of the Haun and Acarseid anchorages in Eriskay but came away empty-handed.

The second boat still on the loose had an almost symbolic significance. It was the boat which had been intercepted to the north of Barra by local police back in April. It had contained the only men from Barra to be brought to book over the *Politician* affair, and the very first to be prosecuted. Unfortunately, McColl and Gledhill knew nothing about the boat – its name, registration, owner or anything which might have helped them locate it. Optimistically, Gledhill called the police sergeant in Castlebay on 21 June, four days before his

planned trip to collect the Eriskay boat, asking him to identify and seize the offending vessel. The sergeant concurred and
put down the telephone.

Four days later Gledhill found himself in the southern isles,
at the end of what should have been a triumphant day, without
a smack from Eriskay and with no satisfactory reply from the
police in Barra. Gledhill went back to Skye and returned to
Lochboisdale on 4 July. There was still no sign of either boat. On
the following day, he reported, "I phoned the police sergeant in
Barra, who then informed me that he could not now identify
the boat."

The feelings of the customs men for the Inverness-shire police
force had cooled over the past few months. They had progressed
from commending young constables for their sterling work to
muttering obliquely about the lack of police will to see this
campaign through to its bitter end. Now they began to regard
the police almost as accomplices after the act. It was, on Ivan
Gledhill's part, a desperate mistake.

He began to snipe at the police in correspondence and in
official reports. When a police constable in Benbecula found a
man drunk in charge of an RAF lorry at nine in the morning, he
asked Charles McColl to take a hydrometer reading of the
strength of the whisky found in the man's possession. McColl
did so, found it to be extremely strong and reported to Gledhill
his suspicion that it had been part of the *Politician's* cargo.
Gledhill promptly wrote to his superiors to complain that the
police had omitted to notify the Excise of their finding "looted,
uncustomed spirits". This appeared, he added damningly, "to be
another case in which the police have failed to comply with
Section 206, Customs Consolidation Act". Reporting back to
base on the original cause of the looting of the *Politician*,
Gledhill suggested that police action could have nipped the

whole affair in the bud. "The co-operation of the police in its prevention," he said, "left much to be desired."

Finally Ivan Gledhill took the bull by the horns. On 5 August he wrote to the Chief Constable of Inverness-shire, William Fraser, to complain that the police had not formally notified the Commissioners of Customs and Excise in London of the exact amount of whisky seized and held in Lochboisdale police station.

This was too much. Fraser was a patient man, but not one to suffer fools, even in the uniform of a Customs and Excise surveyor. He replied to Gledhill:

> In view of the fact that an excise officer was present in nearly every instance in which goods were taken possession of by the police, formal notification to the commissioners was not considered necessary. Such goods of course remain in police possession until the date of trial, after which they are technically in the possession of the court until disposed of, the result of which I shall let you have in due course.
>
> Meanwhile can you please inform me how they are to be taken over if it should be decided that the goods are to be handed to the commissioners. In these matters as you are probably aware, the police act under instructions from the Crown through the Procurator-Fiscal.

Gledhill failed to take the hint. He was consumed by professional angst at the thought of the easy circulation of undutied whisky, particularly among the well-paid, hard-drinking labourers at Balivanich airstrip. Stories were rife in the islands about lorryloads of whisky being driven up the rough and undulating single track between Lochboisdale and Benbecula. On one celebrated occasion an RAF truck had found itself pursued by the police. The truck's driver sped into Balivanich ahead of the law, veered sharply on to the landing strip and dumped its precious load in the path of a bulldozer which was busy levelling sections of newly laid tar. Occasionally men would be found in possession of suspect whisky – often decanted into another bottle – but charges were never brought against them. With salvors busy emptying the *Politician* of her remaining whisky and with a good part of the small boat fleet of South Uist immobilised, with men in prison and with the voice of the law a strangely hollow voice in the southern isles, the Inverness-shire constabulary was inclined to call it a day.

But Ivan Gledhill was not. Where the cargo of the *Politician* was concerned he was as Captain Ahab and the whisky his great white whale. The seizures of individual bottles of whisky in Benbecula, along with suitable police evidence, would, he wrote to his immediate superior, the Collector in Inverness, "be ample to secure a conviction on *revenue charges*". Unfortunately, he went on, the cases:

> . . . have not as far as I can ascertain been the subject of any police charge . . . I would strongly urge that action be taken on these cases, and also . . . against any similar offenders . . . from all information I could gather in my recent visit to the islands I am satisfied that there is a steady flow of unearthed, buried looted spirits from South Uist and Eriskay to Benbecula by aerodrome lorries, and in my opinion salutory action is necessary.

Chief Constable William Fraser took this badly. He decided to point out to the customs authorities that the police did have other work to do and that their services were not exactly cost-free. He wrote to Gledhill's employers, the Commissioners of Customs and Excise in London, reminding them of the two mainland police sergeants he had sent to Eriskay, at the request of Ivan Gledhill, in June. "This involved the police in some expense," said Fraser, "and I should indeed be grateful to know if the expense could be met out of customs funds."

Not surprisingly, Fraser received no early reply from London to this unlikely request. Two weeks later he pressed home his advantage. On 14 October he wrote again to the Commissioners, this time extending his demands from them: "So far I do riot appear to have received your reply to my letter, and I should be grateful if early consideration could be given to the question of expenses referred to." William Fraser then brought his trump into play:

Considerable quantities of uncustomed goods are lying in our police station at Lochboisdale. There is no suitable place in Lochboisdale for storing such goods and because of them full use of the station is being denied to me. In Lochboisdale at the present time this is a serious matter because of the pressure which their duties impose on the police officers stationed there. On 18th August 1941 I wrote to your surveyor in Portree (Ivan Gledhill) suggesting that the goods at Lochboisdale be removed by the salvage vessel *Assistance* which was then at Lochboisdale in connection with the salvaging of goods on the SS *Politician*. The goods could be shipped under the supervision of your local customs officer. This suggestion seems to me a most practical one in view of the fact that there is no customs house in any part of the Outer Hebrides situated in the county of Inverness.

On the same day Fraser, ramming home his advantage, wrote to Gledhill in Portree. He repeated his complaint that the goods stored in Lochboisdale police station, which were putting

Constable Mackenzie under an unimaginable variety of pressures, had not been removed by the salvage vessels. And he invoked the severest possible threat:

> Can you please inform me what the position is? I am afraid some early decision will be required to be made as the goods are now blocking up the police station at Lochboisdale, and their removal is desired as soon as possible in order that we may have the full use of the office.
>
> The delay in dealing with this matter has been rather dreadful, and I am afraid that if there is to be much further delay I must take up the matter with the Secretary of State.

William Fraser did, in time, succeed in getting the whisky removed from his police station, but he was never paid compensation for the use of his men in a customs search. After much agonising and telephoning between London and Portree, the following internal memorandum, circulated within the Commissioners' offices, decided against such a precedent:

> The chief constable has asked for some of the expense incurred by the police in tracking smugglers of goods from the wreck to be met out of customs funds. Little can be said in favour of this application. There are numerous grounds for refusal, the principal of which are: The chief constable required considerable prodding before he complied with his statutory duties under S206 of the Sea Act 1876, and then in many cases it was too late to be of service to our officers in collaboration with the police. The local police do not appear to have actively co-operated with our officers in the detection of smugglers . . .

"Prodding"? "Smugglers"? It did not matter – William Fraser had achieved his objective. He had got Ivan Gledhill off his back.

It took the Procurator-Fiscal a little longer. There was now a new man behind that desk. Immediately after the trials in June interim Procurator-Fiscal John Gray had left to fulfil a long-term ambition – he had joined the RAF. He was replaced in the job which covered, for the Crown prosecution service, the courts both in Portree and in Lochmaddy, by a young man who came from Breakish in Skye and who had been practising in Glasgow. Donald Macmillan had hardly been a week at his new post before he was under pressure from Ivan Gledhill to press extra charges against men found in possession of suspect whisky, and also against the four people who had been collared during the combined police/Excise raid on Eriskay in June. Macmillan asked Gledhill to get his Commissioners' opinion on the matter. Gledhill applied to London. The result swept the rug, finally, from under his feet. Gledhill wrote to Macmillan at the end of October:

> With reference to the seizure of uncustomed spirits and other goods, ex-SS *Politician,* by police and excise officers on Eriskay Island on 5th-7th June last and subsequent seizures by police, I am to inform you that the Honourable the Commissioners of Customs and Excise do not desire that proceedings under the Customs Consolidation Act be taken in these cases against the alleged offenders.

Ever hopeful, he added:

> I should however be glad to be informed for the information of the Commissioners whether you contemplate other

proceedings in these cases and whether subsequently you will be good enough to inform me of the results of such cases.

Macmillan saw his escape route, and groped towards it. He replied:

In all cases of theft from the above vessel where there was sufficient evidence the accused was charged with theft. I have asked Crown Counsel whether such cases be reported to the Customs authorities and was informed that the common law charge of theft alone would be preferred, and that no other steps would be taken.

This was not precise enough for Gledhill. There was still the question of the four Eriskay men who had been discovered, at great cost to the police and to the Crown, to have whisky from the *Politician* hidden on their crofts. He asked:

Will you kindly inform me whether it is intended to take any proceedings against any or all of [the four men] ... If proceedings have taken place or are to be taken in the future in these or other similar cases involving seizure by the police of uncustomed goods subsequent to June 7th, I would be obliged if you would be so good as to inform me in due course of the results of such proceedings.

This was a different Ivan Gledhill, writing with the stiff, strained courtesy of a man who does not really expect a satisfactory reply. He was right. Macmillan immediately answered:

In the cases of [two of the men] I find that my predecessor decided to take no proceedings. In the cases of [the other two] it was discovered that these men had left their homes and gone to sea immediately after the stolen property was found in their possession. I have been informed that [one of them] is at the moment in the neighbourhood and if this information is correct I intend proceeding against him on a common charge of theft.

But Donald Macmillan never did proceed with that common charge of theft. The authorities in the Highlands and Islands, not to say London, were heartily sick of the tawdry business of the SS *Politician*. Nobody else from the southern isles was to gain a criminal record as the result of their association with the stricken ship.

As the affair died, slowly and grumpily, of ignominy, even the small boats were returned. Gledhill received word from London to authorise McColl to resell the vessels to their owners for the best price available. This he did, accepting graciously that while the Excise might get more for them on the open market, it was possibly better that they remain in South Uist – "despite the possible greater potential value of the boats, no greater net yield is possible than that which will be obtained by him [McColl]".

As the men of the southern isles returned, one by one, to the water, to place and to haul their lobster pots, to attend to their livestock on offshore grazing islands; as the owners of the boats that got away in Barra and in Eriskay began slowly to feel safe enough to put to sea again; as people returned from prison in Inverness bearing the news that it had not been all that bad, that they had been treated well and spent their time, not in cells sewing mailbags, but in the hospital ward or the prison garden; as bottles uncovered from artful hiding places were opened and toasts drunk to Captain Beaconsfield Worthington of the SS *Politician*, life in the southern isles of the Outer Hebrides returned, that autumn of 1941, to something like normality. What one old lady from Eriskay was to describe later as "the happiest year in my life – we had so much fun out of it" was coming to an end.

Only the huge hulk in the glittering Sound of Eriskay remained, by now almost part of the landscape, like a newly born volcanic island in Icelandic waters. But the life of the SS *Politician* and the story of her cargo was not yet over.

SEVEN

To the Bottom of the Sea

An ceann na bliadhna a dh'innseas an t-iasgair iasgach.
It is at the end of the year that the fisherman tells of his fishing
– Hebridean saying

Throughout the summer of 1941 Captain Edward Lauretson steadily emptied the holds of the wrecked *Politician,* preparing her for the day when Percy Holden and his divers would pump her clean of oil and water, seal her shattered bulkheads, fill her with compressed air, attach her to tugs and attempt to float her again, all the way back to Clydeside.

By September the 13,093 cases and three casks of whisky, one cask of beer and one cask of sherry which had been hauled out of Hold Number Five and pronounced redeemable, had all been shipped, under hatches sealed by the Customs and Excise, on coasters and lighters to the railheads of Troon and Ardrossan on the south-west coast of Scotland.

Hold Number Five was not completely emptied. Divers reported, when they had completed their operations, that "one stack of probably about 2,000 cases of spirits and, on the bottom of the hold, a very large accumulation of loose paper, carton cases and loose bottles, both broken and unbroken" remained among the water, oil, and tidal detritus. Charles McColl later amended these figures to between 3,000 and 4,000 cases of whisky, with "thousands" of loose bottles. He estimated that the people of the southern isles had made away with about 2,000 cases, or 24,000 bottles, worth roughly £15,000 in lost revenue.

From Troon and Ardrossan the salvaged whisky was put into locked railway carriages, sealed once again by excisemen and transported to Kilmarnock. At no stage in its extraordinary, circuitous transit had the cargo of the SS *Politician* been free from interference and this last journey home was no exception. The crews of the coasting vessels showed scant respect for the Crown seal. One crew in particular was so extravagant in its indulgence that the master and his men were prosecuted on the mainland. In court they pleaded that the whisky found in their possession had not been taken from their own hold, but had in fact been lifted directly from the SS *Politician* while they were alongside her, loading. Their plea was accepted, and the case against them was dismissed. The tattered split standards which had accompanied the cargo of the *Politician* from Liverpool docks to the Traigh Mhor in Barra, to South Glendale, to Royal Naval vessels in Loch Boisdale, to Balivanich airstrip and to Lochmaddy Sheriff Court stayed with it to the end.

Sealed railway carriages were found to be broken and unlocked upon their arrival in Kilmarnock. Cases were found to have "collapsed in transit", and "bottles were found lying loose". By the time the torn and violated shipment reached warehouses in Glasgow, Dundee, Leith and Queensferry – the very warehouses from which, nine months earlier, Secretary of State Johnston had demanded they be removed and sold to America – the customs men who had followed the seductive bottles every step of the way were on the point of giving up. "We do not consider that in the circumstances," an official, conclusive report determined, "a duty charge on the basis of the original contents of all relanded cases can be maintained." Ordinarily the excisemen would have insisted on duty being paid on all shortages known to have arisen after salvage. In the case of the cargo of the *Politician* they were almost past caring and the duty on bottles which went missing between the Sound of Eriskay and Kilmarnock was simply written off.

Back in that sound the *Politician* was, by 22 September, judged ready to float again. Her holds had been sufficiently emptied, the tides were appropriately high and the day dawned fine. She was pumped full of enough air to sail a barrage balloon, hawsers from the salvage boat *Marauder* were attached to her stern and, with Percy Holden, Edward Lauretson, Charles McColl and Ivan Gledhill watching from the deck of the *Assistance* like the occupants of a patrons' box on opening night, the *Marauder*'s cables squealed tight and the old ship rumbled, inch by inch, into the Sound.

Miraculously the *Politician* floated again. But at this point an extraordinary argument broke out on the deck of the *Assistance*. Should she continue immediately on her voyage to Lochboisdale, riding her luck and a benign sea, where she could be secured again until larger vessels came to tow her to Rothesay, or should she be spared at this stage the risks of the Minch and be simply grounded elsewhere in the Sound of Eriskay so that further work could be done? In the end the latter opinion prevailed and the *Politician* was moved a few hundred yards to a sand-bank near the shore of South Uist. There she was settled, only to wallow upon an invisible rock and strike another bulk-head. She was hauled away again, the air was released from her holds and she sank with the hopes and expectations of Holden, Lauretson, McColl and Gledhill on to a smooth area of the bottom of the sea.

Another salvage vessel, the *Caroline Moller,* was sent to her from Loch Ewe and the representatives of another company,

J. B. Cousins, arrived to look her over early in October. They found the *Politician* "badly damaged from the after bulkhead of the engine room to the stern frame. She was tidal in the machinery space and Numbers Four, Five, and Six Holds. The stern frame and rudder were wrenched off and parts missing, while the tail shaft, propeller and stern tube were lying on the bottom."

The cost of dragging her back to dry dock and effecting enough repairs to put her into service again was now estimated at £100,000. Like Commander Kay, the Harrison Lines and a clutch of underwriters before them, the British Iron and Steel Corporation (Salvage) Ltd gave up on the idea of relaunching the ship.

Mournfully the seamen, the engineers, the divers and the customs officers departed the scene. And then the Hebridean weather, which had smiled upon the *Politician* with unusual kindness for nine months, turned against her. Between 8 and 10 November violent gales and storms tossed the ship off her resting place. She was pounded by heavy seas and hammered against the seabed, she was jogged and shunted, for a third and final time, by the uncontrollable elements along the Sound of Eriskay and put down where she still remains, a long, long way from the Mississippi Delta and the Blue Mountains of Jamaica. Divers were sent to her one more time, to cut holes in her forward shell plating – the only part of the ship which was still seaworthy and watertight, and which was helping to keep her partly buoyant – and the SS *Politician* was scuttled in shallow water.

The salvage authorities reverted to Plan B. They began to assess the best way of getting as much metal and as many workable parts off the ship. They decided to cut her into two and remove her more serviceable forward half, as intact as was possible, to Rothesay. The stern half would remain in the Sound of Eriskay to be picked at by engineers, divers . . . and excisemen.

The nine-month nightmare of Charles McColl and Ivan Gledhill was not yet over. The stern half, the half which was to remain at the mercy of the seas and oxyacetylene torches, included, of course, Hold Number Five. Plated up and stamped with the customs seal, Hold Number Five still contained the equivalent of as many as 4,000 cases of whisky. The last salvage vessel, the *Attendant,* which the authorities intended to use to remove the troublesome stuff, had already been despatched to Troon. Only one course of action remained to Ivan Gledhill if he was to relieve himself of this intractable cargo. He spoke at length to Edward Lauretson and to Percy Holden and then he wrote to his immediate superior, the collector in Inverness. Gledhill recommended to Inverness that the customs authorities, if they were to rid themselves finally and forever of the burdensome whisky, must resort to a kind of maritime version of the King's Pipe. The King's Pipe was a device familiar to excisemen, if not to the general public. It was the ironic nickname for the furnace into which customs officials had, since time immemorial, thrown confiscated goods for which they could find no other use. Smuggled laces and perfume from France, silks from the Orient and furs from the distant Caucasus had found their way, in the past, into the King's Pipe. It put a neatly profitless end to their transit. Obviously, the King's Pipe was yet to be built which could take the remnants of an 8,000-ton merchant steamer, even a somewhat battered 8,000-ton merchant steamer; so Ivan Gledhill wrote to Inverness:

> If "piecemeal" salvage of the *Politician* is proceeded with, the Salvage Officials have promised that the removal of all dutiable and drawback cargo will have their first attention.
>
> I am informed that it may be impracticable to remove all the bottles and glass from the bottom of Number Five, but in

this event a sufficient number of charges of explosives of sufficient size will be detonated there to ensure that there will be
no possibility of any unbroken bottles remaining.

Approval is respectfully requested for this course to be
adopted should it be decided by the salvage authorities that
removal is impracticable.

*"To ensure that there will be no possibility of any unbroken
bottles remaining"* – from the man who had accused the people
of the Uists, Barra, and Eriskay of wanton vandalism . . . but
Gledhill got his approval. The Collector in Inverness applied to
London, who in turn consulted the ships' underwriters, and he
received back a brief note. "If the salvage officials find it impracticable," the memo read, "to remove the dutiable goods in
Number Five Hold, these goods may be destroyed by explosive
charge."

It did not happen immediately, this final solution. All
salvage operations were suspended for the winter of 1941–2
and did not resume until the following April. Throughout that
spring and summer McColl brooded over the ship as she was
painstakingly sliced into two neat halves. At the beginning of
August 1942 her forward section was taken off to Rothesay
and her aft end had been cut down to the low water level of
spring tides. McColl nudged Percy Holden, the latter agreed
to honour his pledge and McColl was able to write to London
on 27 August 1942:

Any dutiable cargo remaining on board was demolished on
6th August, when 16 sticks of gelignite were used. I attended
the demolition in company with the salvage officer, who
assured me that no spirits on board would survive the blast-
ing of the gelignite . . . Assuming that any dutiable cargo in

the nature of bottled spirits survived the blowing up, I am
satisfied that it could not be removed except by a diver in
diving gear.

Divers in diving gear were at a premium in the villages of the
southern isles. The *Politician*'s cargo seemed, at last, to be safe
from marauding hands. The islanders were left to watch and to
ponder on the sanity of their public servants. "Dynamiting
whisky," commented Angus John Campbell. "You wouldn't
think there'd be men in the world so crazy as *that*!"

Sporadic salvaging of steel from the *Politician* continued
throughout the Second World War and the ship was not finally
left at peace until the July of 1944. But Charles McColl and Ivan
Gledhill at last felt free to pen their final reports in the autumn
of 1942. "Assuming that 3,000 cases remained on board," wrote
McColl, who was never able to reach an entirely satisfactory
assessment of the number of bottles of whisky that he had
submitted to an underwater explosion, "and that most of the
cartons were destroyed, there remains a discrepancy of over 2,000
cases and these must be regarded as having been pilfered . . .":

The question of placing watchmen on the ship was proposed
by me to Commander Kay of the original salvage team before
his departure, and his verdict was that it was quite impracticable, giving as his reasons the position of the ship, the time
of the year, and the fact that a gale of wind might easily cause
her to break in half and settle in deep water, with the highly
probable loss of any person or persons on board. During the
time of his own salvage operations he left no watchmen on
board for the same reasons.

The fact that there were no watchmen on board, together
with the fact that the ship was stranded on a rock eight miles

from Lochboisdale, simplified matters for looters who took full advantage of their opportunities. A request for assistance by the Police Constable was turned down, so that the oversight of the wreck devolved on one Customs and Excise officer and one Police Constable eight miles from the ship . . .

There is no doubt that a considerable quantity of the looted spirits were disposed of to workmen engaged on various public works contracts in the islands of South Uist and Benbecula, and that a considerable quantity was sent outwith the islands by Parcel Post. In the latter connection authority was requested from the Post Office to examine outgoing parcel mail of Lochboisdale Post Office, through which office all the island mail circulates; but no such authority was granted. It is understood that in one case the local Postmaster was asked to detain any suspected parcel and I gather that the attitude of the official was to broadcast the fact that he had been so instructed, and I am also strongly of the opinion that his instructions to detain were completely disregarded.

With proper facilities at their disposal, Charles McColl concluded, the excisemen could have operated in such a way that "practically all the looting would have been prevented".

Ivan Gledhill, in his last word to London, agreed with McColl that a motor boat patrol or a shore watch could have protected the *Politician*'s cargo. He added:

So far as can be estimated there has been a loss of about 2,000 cases of whisky by looting. The co-operation of the Police in its prevention left much to be desired . . . Cargo was badly stained and damaged by fuel oil, which covered everything and rendered identification of markings here impossible.

Tallying under these conditions was difficult, and was rendered more so by the need for haste in getting packages into coastal hatches . . .

From my visits to the vessel and from conversations with salvage officers and with divers I agree with the officer [McColl] as to the quantities remaining in the hold when salvage operations ceased. I am satisfied that these were effectively destroyed by the explosion amongst them of 16 sticks of gelignite, approval for which action had been obtained previously.

I agree with the officer that some 2,000 cases of spirits were looted, and this estimate agrees with our estimate formed at and immediately subsequent to the looting epidemic. There is little doubt that practically all this has gone into consumption, largely by sale amongst aerodrome construction gangs and partly by being forwarded to mainland acquaintances of the islanders.

Of the casks of whisky and beer unaccounted for, some are known to have been destroyed in the wreck and salvage operations, and the contents lost, and as there has been no rumour or suspicion of any casks being looted I am of the opinion that the remainder have been similarly destroyed. The cases of stout and sherry have been indistinguishable from those containing whisky on account of fuel oil contamination, and in respect of any uncovered it cannot be established whether they have been looted or destroyed.

No cases of cigarettes or tobacco have been identified here. Cigarettes were amongst the seizures and packets of them at one time littered the paths of Eriskay island, but they were spoiled by fuel oil and seawater. If block or plug tobacco, or cigarettes in airtight tins (e.g. 50s) were amongst that looted, such probably went into consumption. Small, airtight tin packings should have prevented contamination of their contents.

Of the . . . artificial silk and cotton tissues one bale at least, badly stained by fuel oil, was used by the salvage people as cleaning rags . . .

There was a brief footnote to these last, sad communications. On 30 September 1942, Charles McColl called at Lochboisdale police station and removed ten cases of whisky and two boxes, containing 144 bottles and one half bottle, 20 months after he had first seized them and entrusted them to the nervous care of PC Donald Mackenzie and 13 months after Chief Constable William Fraser had threatened to invoke the Scottish Secretary to effect their removal. They were taken by the SS *Assistance* to Castlebay in Barra and from there by steamer to Troon. They were strapped tightly with wire and stamped with the customs seal.

Ivan Gledhill moved on from Skye after the war, travelling to live in Kenya before settling happily in retirement in a remote part of the Lancashire countryside.

Charles McColl spent the rest of his life in South Uist. He retired in 1949, at the age of 60, and died two years later from a coronary thrombosis. His wife was to claim that the affair of the *Politician* killed him. The post of Customs and Excise Officer in Lochboisdale which was left vacant by his retiral was never filled. From 1949 onwards, the whole of the southern isles came under the auspices of the Customs House at Stornoway in the Island of Lewis, 80 sea miles north of the Sound of Eriskay and, in the opinion of many, eight years too late.

So Charles McColl did not live to see the most mysterious incident to follow in the broad wake of the SS *Politician,* although he would have been aware of its origins. Those little scraps of paper which divers kept coming across in the sticky depths of Hold Number Five, those worthless Jamaican bank-notes, floated ominously to the surface. They had been nothing more than an irrelevance to the customs men and to the salvors. There was no duty payable on them, and they were not, in Great Britain, legal tender. In 1941 it was surely inconceivable that any inhabitant of the Outer Hebrides could have put them to good use. De La Rue could easily run off a few thousand more, and so they were shovelled to one side.

The salvage engineer Percy Holden of Arnott Young came across a few on Eriskay one day. While strolling around he found a group of small children playing shops with the notes. "They come in on the sea," they told him. Holden alerted his divers to this, and they eventually unearthed, beneath bales of cloth and crates of whisky in Hold Number Five, a tin box which contained £360,000 in Jamaican ten shilling notes. He posted them to Arnott Young, who handed them over to the Bank of England. The Old Lady of Threadneedle Street, for her part, sent Holden a letter of thanks.

But there was more, much more, in circulation – and not only in the southern isles where children have been brought up playing monopoly with the Jamaican currency. In 1941 an RAF corporal was arrested in Rothesay trying to change Jamaican currency. He produced evidence of having spent time in the West Indies and was acquitted.

In December 1952 the *Sunday Dispatch* splashed an unusual story. "Banknotes, part of a cargo of £250,000-worth printed in London for Jamaica and written off as lost in a shipwreck in 1941, have suddenly appeared over the counters of shops and bars in the West Indian Colony," revealed the newspaper.

The authorities want to know how they got there. A Colonial Office spokesman told me: "We have received information from Jamaica and it has been placed in the hands of Scotland Yard. The new notes were sent from London on the steamship *Politician* in February 1941. They never reached Jamaica because the ship was wrecked."

The ten shilling and one pound notes, all dark blue, were fresh from the presses of the De La Rue company, which prints currency for half the countries of the world.

Lloyds of London told me: "The *Politician* was caught in a violent storm off the Outer Hebrides, Scotland, forced on to the rocks, and badly holed. The order was given to abandon her. As far as we know all the cargo, including the fortune in notes, was left aboard. We have no record of her ultimate end. Some time after she had been abandoned an attempt was made to refloat her, but she broke in half. She was left as a wreck. By now she may have been battered to pieces, or may still be lying there, half-submerged. We presume the crew escaped, probably by being taken off by another vessel. As far as we know there was no heavy loss of life."

Banks were notified that the cargo had been lost and given the numbers of the banknotes for cancellation. Now bank managers in Jamaica find the cancelled notes in circulation. They are asking how the money, last heard of in sealed steel boxes in the strong-room of the *Politician,* could have travelled 4,000 miles from the rocks of the Outer Hebrides.

Three theories are offered to explain the re-emergence of the notes: Looters may have boarded the *Politician* after she had been abandoned, found the notes and kept them in store until they could be disposed of profitably. The steel boxes containing them might have been washed ashore, found by beachcombers, and later transferred to the underworld. Some of the money may have been salvaged by the crew and taken to safety but not given up. The Security Branch of the

Colonial Office are checking up on original members of the crew of the *Politician*.

The following day's *Daily Mail* pursued the *Dispatch*'s story. It reported:

> Last night an hotel-keeper at Pollachar, South Uist, nearest the spot to the site of the wreck, told me that the whisky-looters who boarded the *Politician* "brought back thousands of pounds of money". The notes were in good condition, but from what he remembered the islanders destroyed their haul, thinking it worthless.
>
> "There was some report that a quantity of it went abroad, but where to and how I don't know," he said. Police of South Uist and neighbouring Barra knew nothing about the money and so far have not been contacted by Scotland Yard.

The notes continued to crop up, often passed through the hands of Messrs Thomas Cook, until 1957, and the stories surrounding them multiplied and grew taller. Men are supposed to have made the journey to the West Indies in order to convert enormous quantities of notes into less culpable currency. Houses and small farms are rumoured to have been built from the proceeds. For a number of years the page of the *Politician*'s manifest which included the De La Rue consignment was concealed from public eyes – presumably as a relic of wartime security – and this only fed the flame of rumour. The *Politician* was a mystery ship, it was claimed, carrying bizarre quantities of hard cash and harder liquor for nefarious purposes in the West Indies. An alternative Buckingham Palace was to be established in the Caribbean; the Duke and Duchess of Windsor, then resident in the Bahamas, demanded such supplies; Errol Flynn, who was, for a while, in Jamaica during the Second World War, had to be paid off to stop his flirting with Nazis . . . the afterlife of the *Politician* has been a wildly glamorous thing since Compton Mackenzie seized his opportunity to base possibly the best – and certainly the best-selling – Scottish comic novel on the diverting junket which took place on the islands and sounds around his house in the early years of the Second World War.

Oddly, Compton Mackenzie heard nothing at the time about the missing money. During the "Plundered Notes Turning Up In Jamaica" scare of 1952 a journalist telephoned him at his Edinburgh home and was surprised to learn that the author "hadn't known that the *Politician* had been carrying money. He thinks it must have been in the strongroom, which 'the boys' left alone."

"They found some stout," said Compton Mackenzie, "but they weren't interested in that. They found some printed frocks, but they weren't interested in those. The only things they wanted were the whisky and a piano for the schoolroom. But they couldn't get the piano ashore."

Whoever took the bank-notes Sir Compton is sure it wasn't the islanders. "If it was I would have heard about it," he said.

Which only goes to show that the affectionately regarded author was not privy to *all* of the secrets of his adopted Hebridean community. In which case, what hope has anybody else?

It was never very likely that the *Politician,* even as a shattered, twisted and sawn-off hulk which no longer even broke the surface of the Sound of Eriskay, would rest in a quiet grave. A blanket of security cocooned the wonderful story of her final voyage throughout the years of the Second World War, but in peacetime the tales and legends began to drift southwards, gathering colour and momentum as the fiction of Compton Mackenzie's *Whisky Galore* was linked to the actual events of 1941. They brought renown of a kind to the people of the southern isles, the reputation of being a friendly, innocent race, proud in an otherworldly sort of way, and with a fondness of – and capacity for – strong drink that was never of this earth. And on the heels of the stories and the romantic reputations, they brought men in diving suits to the Sound of Eriskay.

It is not possible to say with certainty when the first recreational dive to the wreck of the SS *Politician* was made, how many years of peace she enjoyed after Percy Holden's divers lodged their sticks of gelignite and retired to a safe distance. But by the 1960s the bones of the *Politician,* with their allure of famously illicit whisky, had become something of a mecca for British sub-aqua clubs.

In the February of 1966, 25 years to the month after the *Politician* ran aground, a trio of wet-suited and goggled enthusiasts decided upon an anniversary dive. They were a Stornoway hotelier, Ian Davidson, a man called Capaldi who had run a cafe in Lewis until leaving recently with his family to work in Aldershot, and who described himself as an "Italian Gael", and Reg Valentine, a diver of international renown who had his own sub-aqua school on the Island of Zembra, another speck of rock in the warmer waters of the Mediterranean coast of Tunisia.

Valentine was impressed, nonetheless, by diving conditions in the Sound of Eriskay. "This is one of the most interesting dives I have ever undertaken," he said, ". . . pure white sand makes visibility perfect." The three men made a brief, preliminary 15-minute sortie to the wreck and, to their great astonishment, surfaced with four bottles of whisky. The following day they dived again and this time, scraping in the sand and around the rusted spars, they were able to bring up more than 30 bottles. The contents of the bottles proved to be not quite so delightfully pure as the seabed of sand. They were, said Capaldi, "all shapes and sizes of bottles but neither labels nor whisky – only a brew that stank horribly". Oil, salt water and the effulgences of the bottom of the sea had, over a quarter of a century, soaked slowly through the corked caps of the *Politician's* cargo of "millionaire's whisky", rendering it utterly undrinkable, an almost indescribable dark brew of sulphuric rotted matter. The Stornoway customs officers, to whom the three divers obediently delivered their findings, had no difficulty in declaring them free from any burden of payable duty, and the divers took back their bottles to shelves and mantelpieces in Lewis, Aldershot and the Gulf of Tunis. The fact of the stuff being unfit to drink was, declared Reg Valentine, almost irrelevant. He had been swimming in the belly of a relic of modern history, and "I never really thought I would get a souvenir".

From Inverness and Manchester, London and Aberdeen, amateur and professional divers arrived in the seas of the southern isles, and more often than not they went away bearing booty. An Army diving team from the Royal Artillery Range at Benbecula made a dive to the wreck in the 1960s, and surfaced with six bottles which their commanding officer promptly and properly confiscated, locking them in his cellar and writing to HM Customs for advice. The bottles had, he told the men in London, been recovered "during recent training exercises . . . Do you wish us to take any further action in this matter?" After a quick and, no doubt, revelatory flick through the volumes of *Politician* files the customs officials replied that, no, they did not wish any further action to be taken. For them the matter was closed. They no longer cared.

In the late summer of 1987 Donald MacPhee, a native of South Uist who was also a commercial diver, received a telephone call from two English visitors, asking to be shown around the wreck of the ship. This was no problem to MacPhee:

The *Polly* was part of the wallpaper to us in South Uist. It's been on my doorstep from day one. We knew of all the mainland divers who had come over to see her over the years, and all of my family were steeped in stories about the goings-on at the *Politician*. I was first down at her, I think, in 1981, but I've dived there since – particularly in the mid-1980s, when a mussel farm which was being run from Eriskay, and was floating directly above her, was swept away in a storm and we were asked to go down and pick up the pieces.

MacPhee never did recover the mussel farm, but in the course of an extended dive he became familiar with the habitat of the skeletal hulk of the old cargo ship. It was bedded in thin sand, which shifted with every tide and which at some points covered two-thirds of the hull. As the submarine dunes drifted along the floor of the Sound they uncovered and submerged scattered fragments of the *Politician*'s diverse cargo. Like prizes in the sawdust of a lucky-dip barrel, bottles and fragments of glass, telephones, machetes and bolls of calcified linen vanished and reappeared with the surge of the sea and the wandering sand. Donald MacPhee took his two English tourists out to the wreck. "They were determined to get a picture of some sort of the boat," he said.

They kept going on about how the boat was carrying money, and how there was some Windsor connection, curious stories like that. But they were inexperienced divers and after one of them nearly drowned trying to photograph the boat I decided, for their own sakes, on a small deception. I told them that the foredeck of the *Polly* was high and dry on the Uist shore, and I took them over to an old dry dock out by Ru Melvich, past where the *Thala* went down, and they quite happily sat there and took pictures.

They weren't pictures of the *Polly*, but it saved themselves from drowning. Oh, they were very keen.

Back in South Uist Donald MacPhee learned that his two innocents were, in fact, an editor and photographer from an English newspaper, the *Mail on Sunday*, and that they did not intend to give up on the *Politician* easily. He came clean about their first expedition and a week later they asked him again to organise a dive around the wreck. This time an Independent Television News cameraman was present, and this time MacPhee established his rights through the Salvage Association – "Just in case we wanted to take anything off, else we'd have had the Receiver of Wrecks chasing us, the underwriters chasing us, if there was publicity and we hadn't been through the formalities we'd have been in trouble. You don't want to be seen robbing and plundering by those people." He was to be glad that he had taken the trouble.

For ten days MacPhee and a small group of amateur divers delved in the hulk of the *Politician*, with airlift equipment and a winch aboard their support vessel, and when the newspaper and television people had left with their stories Donald MacPhee was left with a bucketful of rusted machetes, the remains of inscribed whisky crates, eight bottles of Scotch, and a deep conviction that down there among the twisted spars and festoons of seaweed there was much, much more. Struck by the notion that the bottles might be worth money he asked the fine art auctioneers Christie's to put them up for public bidding. Christie's agreed and "that was when the whole business of this big old whisky wreck which I'd known about since childhood, stopped being a joke".

Christie's auctioned the eight bottles at the Assembly Rooms in Edinburgh on 11 November 1987. They divided them into six lots, two of two bottles and four of one, and asked for bids upwards of £250 per bottle. Donald MacPhee thought this to be highly optimistic: "We were thinking that if the sale of them covered our costs down to Edinburgh we'd be doing well." The first bottle, Lot 271 – "Bottled by W. & A. Gilbey. Original cork. Wax sealed by Christie's. Plain glass bottle. Shoulder embossing states 'Federal law forbids sale or re-use of this bottle' " – went under the hammer at £572. Lot 272 – a pair of the same – sold for £1,155. Lot 273, a green Ballantine bottle, tempted a final bid of £605. And Lot 274, a brown glass Peter Dawson screw-top, heard the tap of the mallet at £660. Donald MacPhee left the Assembly Rooms with £4,000 and a busy mind.

A full-scale salvage of the wreck of the *Politician* was, he decided, inevitable. The legend of *Whisky Galore* haunted the vessel and, as the years passed, showed no signs of evaporating. "If I didn't do it," he reflected, "somebody else would have a bash." In consultation with his accountant, a businessman from Skye called Neil Campbell who operated a small sub-office in the southern isles, MacPhee slowly exhausted all of the usual financial institutions. It was simply too risky a proposal for any bank to contemplate investment. Campbell then contacted another business associate, a commercial finance broker from Perth named Mike Bell, who in turn brought in a director of the Glasgow financial services company Churchill Baron, Jeremy Brough, and the four of them formed the SS *Politician* plc.

"Churchill Baron were interested in getting involved in public share issues," Brough explained, "and although this was an unusual kind of issue everybody that we spoke to about it, the solicitors and the accountants to the issue, had such a natural enthusiasm for the project that we believed, ultimately correctly, that we would get a good response from the public."

SS *Politician* plc was launched in Glasgow in October 1989. Its function was to raise at least 500,000 one pound shares, from a minimum individual subscription of £500 per investor. The half-a-million pounds would be used not to raise the hull of the vessel itself, which would be shifted 50 feet from its resting place, but to evacuate a huge hole in the seabed and suction-pump its contents aboard a large support vessel – a cross, in fact, between an archaeological dig and panning for gold. Anything discovered, from bottles of sulphuric whisky and Jamaican ten-shilling notes (valued by Christie's, in mint condition, at between £20 and £30) to the humblest machete, would be sold. The company would also market the name of the ship, riding on the publicity engendered by its own activities, to film and video companies, bottlers of whisky and anybody else who might be interested. Investment in the company, speculators were warned, must be regarded as "involving a degree of risk".

It was as strange a public company as can ever have been launched. The *Politician* was no medieval barque, attacked by Barbary pirates or trapped in a murderous squall and sent to the bottom with its shining cargo. It was not the flagship of an admiral or a monarch, it contained no great artefacts, or secrets of its time, it was host to no imperial memories. The *Politician* was an old and troublesome 8,000-ton merchantman, cut up for scrap and blasted into tangled metal by weary Government officials less than 50 years before. Who would want to risk £500 to send a team of divers to meddle in her hold?

Brough, MacPhee, Campbell and Bell spent just £5,000 on advertising the issue. They had no need to spend more: the world's media took care of that. The words "Whisky Galore" rang cheerful bells from Tokyo to Toronto, it was as if the international press, denied a glorious story in the spring and summer of 1941, were anxious to make up lost ground. Applications for the company's prospectus came in from Hong Kong, Brussels, Thailand, the USA, Canada, Singapore and the Falkland Islands. In all, 7,000 people responded to the publicity, of whom, by February 1990, 580 had invested, leaving the SS *Politician* plc £100,000 short of its £500,000 minimum. The directors cut the share issue by that amount, reissued the prospectus at £403,000, and were able to announce that the final, most troublesome, most expensive and most publicised salvage operation on the ship would go ahead between July and August 1990. The romancing of the *Politician* had found, yet again, a receptive public.

EIGHT

The Fillums

I think it's become, if I may say so, a kind of folk tale.
Rather like Dick Whittington or Aladdin or something.
Because it goes on and on . . . that's the fantastic thing, really, if
you come to think about it.
— Sir Compton Mackenzie

Fittingly, the first people to busy themselves romancing the legend of the *Politician* were the inhabitants of the southern isles.

Upon their return from Inverness Prison the convicted men devised and improvised a drama which they performed before packed audiences in the school halls of the islands. Jessie MacAulay, who was at the time a newly qualified schoolteacher in the corrugated iron shed that served as a school in South Glendale, remembered the entertainment clearly.

I saw it at Garrynamonie, but I think it was at every school hall in Uist. It began with someone coming into a house with the news of the shipwreck, then they sat discussing it, and a sailor knew she was full of whisky, and they prepared to go off to her.

There was a scene in the *Polly* herself, with them hauling crates up from under the stage and singing songs about it.

The last scene was in prison, with them all sewing mailbags – although in fact everybody knew that they weren't in the cells at all, they were in the hospital ward.

One scene was left out because it would have been too long and the whole show went on for three hours as it was. That was the courtroom scene. They never dramatised the courtroom scene. But they improvised all of the rest. Half of it was never written down, it came so naturally to them.

One of the performers, the same Roderick Campbell who had admitted to Procurator-Fiscal Gray that he had indeed been aboard the *Politician,* when she was docked in Vancouver in the late 1920s and his brother Angus John was serving on her, wrote a song commemorating the events. The song, *Oran na Politician,* was later collected and anthologised by the folklorist Margaret Fay Shaw:

1

Thàinig bat' air tìr dha'n àit'
A dh'fhàg mise fo mhìngean,
Fhuair mi aiste dram no dhà,
'S e sin a dh'fhàg cho tinn mi;
Mar a tha mi 'n diu cho truagh,
Cha ghluais mi ach le dichioll;
'S e na dh'òl mi dha'n Spey Royal
Chuir am bròn air m'inntinn.

2

Chuala mi gun robh i ann,
'S gu robh an t-am dhol innte;
Gu robh stuth innte gu leòr,
Bha brògan agus sìod' ann,

Bha uisge beatha mar bha an còrr
Gach brand is seòrs' bha sgrìobhte;
'S ged bha 'n ola dhubh gu h-àrd,
Bha chuid a b'fheàrr gu h-ìseal.

3

Chaidh mi suas mar rinn càch
'S gun chaith sinn pàirt a bh'innte,
Dùil liom nach biodh guth gu bràch air,
Gu robh am bàta millte;
Ach cha b'ann mar sin a bhà
Chaidh brath gun dàil a dh'innse,
'S ann fhuair mi sumaineadh bha garbh
'Gam thoirt air falbh dha'n phrìosan.

4

'S a Loch nam Madadh chaidh sinn sìos
'Gar cur an iarainn cinnteach;
Cha b'e seachdain 's cha b'e mìos,
'S ann gheobhainn bliadhna phrìosan;
Bha 'n Géidseir 's polisman no dhà
An àird air son ar diteadh,
Ach a dh'aindheoin an cuid beòil
'S ann gheobhadh Ròidseag clear.

5

Is ged a dh'fhalbhainn as a siod
Do dh'Eilear Nis dha'n phrìosan,
'S mi nach cromadh sìos mo cheann
Cha bhiodh dad ann do mhìchliù;
'S mur b'e cuid le luas am beòil
'S cho deònach a bhith 'g innse,

Cha d'fhuaras greim air duine riamh
A thug diar air tìr aist'.

6

Ach 's e dh'fhàg mi 'n diu fo ghruaim
'S a chuir an duan air m'inntinn,
Smaointinn air na gillean truagh
Thug a chuairt dha'n phrìosan;
Bha cho onarach 's gach àit',
Cha chluinnt' aig càch am mìomhodh,
'S nach cualas riamh gu robh iad beò
Gu'n bhuail i stròn air tìr ann.

7

Thuirt an Gèidseir an Taigh na Cùirt,' –
'S bha diùmbadh agam fhìn ris –
Gum faigheadh iad i air falbh,
'S nach robh an cargo millte;
'S ged bha mi fhìn air bheagan tùir,
Co dhiù bha fios a'm cinnteach,
Nach gluaiseadh i bho'n chreig gu bràch,
Gur h-ann 'san tràigh a chìt' i.

8

'S ge b'e choisicheas a null
Bho'n Lùdaig 's ann a chì e –
Chì e sealladh dhith le shùil,
'Sa ghrùnnd far bheil i sìnte;
'S e 'm Politician a th'ann,
Car cam innte nach dirich;
'S cha ghluais i as a' siod gu bràch,
Gu'n dèid i mhàin 'na pìosan.

9

Ach nam b'fhiach liom chuirinn sìos e,
'S cha b'e briag a dh'innsinn,
Cuid a fhuair aiste gu leòr
Dha'n h-uile seòrs' a bh'innte;
A bha stràiceil as gach dòigh,
Is leòmach feadh na tìre;
Ach èisdibh mi, 's cha chan mi 'n còrr
Mu'n Pholi chòir gu dìlinn.

Translation

THE SONG OF THE *POLITICIAN*

1. A ship has come ashore in this place, which left me in distress; I got a dram or two out of her; that is what made me so ill; I am so wretched today that I can only move with an effort; the "Spey Royal" I drank has made my mind sorrowful.

2. I heard she was there, and that it was the time to go into her, that there was plenty of stuff in her, there were shoes and silks, and whisky as well, of every known brand; and though there was black (fuel) oil on top, the best part was below.

3. I went up as the rest did, and we used what was in her; I thought that there wouldn't be a word about it, that the ship was a total loss; but that was not how things turned out, a report was made at once, and I got a stern summons, taking me away to prison.

4. We went down to Lochmaddy, expecting to be put in irons; not a week, nor a month, but a year's imprisonment I would get. The Exciseman and a policeman or two were out to condemn us, but in spite of their talk Ròidseag (the author) looked like getting clear.

5. Though I were to go thence to Inverness prison, I would not bow my head, there would be no disgrace in it; but for

some people, with their careless talk and readiness to tell,
not a man who took a drop out of her would have been
caught.

6. What left me sad, and put the poem on my mind, was
thinking of the poor lads whom the Court sent to prison;
who were so well esteemed everywhere, no one was heard
to say they had misbehaved, it hadn't been ever heard they
were alive, until she struck her nose on land there.

7. The Exciseman said in the Court house, and I was annoyed
with him for it, that they would get her away, and that the
cargo was not spoilt; though I was not very intelligent
myself, I knew for sure, at any rate, that she would never
move from the rock, that she would (henceforth) be only
seen ashore.

8. Whoever walks along from Lùdaig will see, will see a sight
of her with his own eyes, where she is stretched out on the
bottom; the *Politician* is there, she has a bend that cannot
be straightened; she'll never move from there until she
goes to pieces.

9. But if it were worth my while, I would put it down, and I
wouldn't tell a lie, some got plenty out of her, of every
kind of thing in her, who were boastful in every way, and
proud throughout the district; but listen to me, and I'll
never say more about the kindly *Polly*.

The *Politician* was not eulogised by all who wrote about her.
When Alastair Alpin MacGregor, a man who had specialised in
glowing, ethereal accounts of the Hebrides throughout his writing career, came to prepare his last book on the subject, titled
simply *The Western Isles* and published after the Second World
War, he turned on the islands with all the fury of an apostate.
MacGregor suddenly found the people whom he had recently

caricatured as quaint, superstitious rustics to be possessed of a superhuman number of vices. Inebriation (more or less permanent inebriation, according to the new MacGregor) was prominent among these sins, and the affair of the *Politician* proof-positive of its contagion.

Alongside the *Politician,* wrote MacGregor,

... hangs a tale of orgy and drunkenness surpassing any in the history of the Outer Hebrides. The drunken condition which the Statutes of Iona sought to assuage early in the seventeenth century was as nothing compared with that which followed the wreck of this vessel ... there now began what some have described as "the greatest Saga of the Outer Hebrides in modern times", but what certain members of the clergy in this locality told me was probably one of the most disastrous episodes in which the islands had ever been involved ...

And so on, and so on ... in condemnation, Alastair Alpin MacGregor was as fluent as he had been in praise. The islanders' "capacity for laziness" was enhanced by this flow of free liquor, Hogarthian scenes of alcoholic squalor littered the *machairs* and the townships, men and women drank themselves to death, and stomach pumps were introduced to the islands by doctors who were themselves much the worse for wear ... It was all so much guff, but MacGregor's lengthy account of the spring and summer of 1941 might have remained as the definitive version, had not a work of pure, sparkling fiction come along to supplant it for ever.

Compton Mackenzie's first taste of the produce of the boat which he was to immortalise as the SS *Cabinet Minister* was brought to him by his driver and mechanic on Barra, Kenny

MacCormack. Word had got around that the people of Eriskay were "accumulating case upon case of whisky" and MacCormack and some other men embarked on a nocturnal expedition from the north end of Barra. "He came back in the morning as black as a crow and exhausted by the night's work down among the cases of whisky in the hold." MacCormack presented Mackenzie with a bag containing six dozen bottles. One of the brands was Grant's Standfast, which Mackenzie enjoyed so much that in later years he would endorse it in advertisements.

Mackenzie was a serious and a prolific writer. Early in the century he had achieved some renown with two novels, *Sinister Street* and *Carnival,* and he had since then pursued the career of a professional writer with a vigour and an appetite which was matched only by his fondness for home-hopping from one island to another. Mackenzie lived on seabound outcrops of rock in the Aegean Sea, on Capri, in the Channel Islands, and finally on Barra in the Outer Hebrides, where he settled in the 1930s and attempted to produce his masterwork among the dunes and the zephyrs which bordered the Traigh Mhor, that tidal cockle strand which still served as an airstrip. Mackenzie would be remembered for a book which originated in Barra, but it was not to be *The Four Winds of Love*.

He had already created a *dramatis personae* of satirical Highland characters in *The Monarch of the Glen,* the first in a series of comic novels which he seemed capable of rattling out in a few weeks' dictation, a cheerful interlude for the writer and his readers alike from the soul-searching of his *magnum opus*. Some of these characters were enlisted when, in 1943, he wrote a light spoof of his time in command of the Barra company of the Second Inverness-shire (West) Battalion of the Local Defence Volunteers. Mackenzie based *Keep the Home Guard Turning* in the southern isles. He adapted the geographical relationship between Barra and its smaller neighbour Vatersay into the twins of Great and Little Todday (Todaidh Mór and Todaidh Beag), and translated the Presbyterian/Catholic division of the northern and southern Outer Isles into this local context. Some of the mainland landowning gentry which had been tickled by his gentle pen in *The Monarch of the Glen,* such as Hector MacDonald of Ben Nevis, were retained in *Keep the Home Guard Turning.* The honeyed style of the first life of Alastair Alpin MacGregor, that gamey writer of Highland travelogues, was once again parodied as Hector Hamish MacKay. ("But hark! What is that melodious moaning we hear in the west? It is the singing of the seals on Poppay and Pillay . . . their fantastic shapes standing out dark against the blood-stained western sky.") And a host of new island parodies were lovingly introduced. Father John MacMillan, the retired parish priest, became Father James MacAlister. The local doctor became Captain Paul Waggett. Some of Mackenzie's friend John (the Coddy) MacPherson's mannerisms, such as the barbarous one of taking lemonade with his whisky, were generously distributed among the characters.

Mackenzie delivered *Keep the Home Guard Turning* to his publishers in the summer of 1943 and informed them at the same time that "I think of following up the HG with the story of the whisky ship wrecked in these parts and call the farce 'Whisky Galore'. Galore is the Gaelic for plenty."

By the December of 1943 *Keep the Home Guard Turning* had become a phenomenal publishing success, going into three impressions within two months. Harold Raymond, Mackenzie's editor at Chatto & Windus, was anxious for more of the same. "I have always liked the sound of 'Whisky Galore' and your Scottish public will like it too," he wrote in 1944. "They positively eat *The Monarch* and *Keep the Home Guard Turning* and can't think why you haven't been more Scottish in the past." But

Mackenzie was deeply involved in his "Four Winds" quartet, and did not get around to writing *Whisky Galore* until the summer of 1946. It was written mainly in Mackenzie's bed at Benchworth in the Vale of the White Horse, the author being struck down by one of the intermittent bouts of severe bad health that dogged his later years. He had left Barra for good in the previous year.

If *Keep the Home Guard Turning* had been a phenomenon, *Whisky Galore* was a success so epic that within a year or two of publication it had dwarfed the rest of Mackenzie's considerable body of published work, made him rich, famous and a Knight, and introduced new popular phrases into both the English and the French languages.

Mackenzie received his first copy of the book in the January of 1948. He was in the Seychelles, considering buying another island home (he did not do so), and starting another Highland novel, *Hunting the Fairies*. By the end of 1949 *Whisky Galore* had sold, in hardback, 33,500 copies, and the publishers were happily turning out a fourth impression. By 1952, when the Reprint Society made it their World Book Choice and ran off 150,000 copies, it had become one of the biggest of post-war bestsellers.

As such it was almost inevitable that the men at Ealing Studios, who were at that time engaged in establishing the nearest that Britain has ever had to a consistently successful indigenous film industry, should take an interest. Mackenzie was still globe-trotting, in Nairobi, when he received, in the May of 1948, a letter telling him that Sir Michael Balcon had agreed to pay £500 for the film rights of *Whisky Galore,* with a further £1,000 if it covered its costs. To Mackenzie, the expense of whose adventurous life had always, until now, exceeded his income, this was a godsend. He later wrote: "People suppose that the film of *Whisky Galore!* made me rich. In fact, the whole amount I made was £2,275 which includes what I was paid for rewriting the script. This may not seem much but the value to me has not been for my purse but for my name." That £2,275 would be, in 2023 value, £68,000.

The film of *Whisky Galore!* was made chiefly as a stop-gap solution to two problems which, in 1948, were niggling the chief producer at Ealing Studios, Michael Balcon. One problem was that his valued head of publicity, Monja Danischewsky, was bored and wanted to leave for Fleet Street; the other was that Balcon had the money to produce an extra film that year, but no available studio space. With the broad sling of a natural mogul, Balcon killed both birds with one stone. Find a film which you can shoot on location, he told the astonished Danischewsky, and you can stay at Ealing as an associate producer.

Danischewsky selected *Whisky Galore* – "It is always easy to be wise after the event, but it astonishes me now that it had not been fought over by film companies from the day it first came out" – received a budget of £60,000, employed a Scottish maker of documentary films, Alexander Mackendrick, to direct his first feature, signed up Basil Radford, Joan Greenwood, Gordon Jackson and Bruce Seton, agreed with Compton Mackenzie that the 65-year-old author could satisfy the ambition of a lifetime by playing Captain Buncher, the fiction's equivalent to Beaconsfield Worthington (Mackenzie had been born into a theatrical family and, while at Oxford, had turned down an acting contract), and in the July of 1948 Danischewsky, the White Russian, Mackendrick, the Presbyterian Scot, and a film crew of 80 arrived on the island of Barra.

For two months Barra became a film set. The crew were billeted with local families, many of them at Northbay, six long miles from the island's only bar at Castlebay. The islanders, despite blinking a little when they saw imitation rocks being levered into place beside the real, native items and the walls of hardboard houses going up on the Traigh Mhor, accepted the "fillums" phlegmatically, many of them cheerfully signing on as extras. They were, for obvious reasons, unfamiliar with the stars of stage and screen and largely unimpressed by their presence. "There was a girl," one woman remembered, "asked if Joan Greenwood was a big star in London. When they said that she was she looked disappointed. 'Doesnae look so smart, does she?' she said. I think she was looking for the glitter and the diamonds, you know . . ."

John Macpherson, the Coddy, appointed himself general factotum to the "fillums". "Transport," recalled Danischewsky, "had to be laid on not when it was required but when it suited him. 'Time was here before you came,' he reproached me once, 'and I daresay time will still be here when you go away again' . . . One never had the last word with the Coddy, but I couldn't have enough of his company." Even when the weather turned bad, there were few sour moments. One or two members of the crew had to be torn away from unpleasant confrontations outside the bar at Castlebay, and Basil Radford, a soft-hearted soul, caused consternation by releasing a flock of sheep which were trussed up at the pier, waiting for the ferry. (Later, moist-eyed and unsteady, he explained: "They were all lying there, the poor sad darlings, bleating their poor little hearts out; I just had to do it . . . if you had seen their eyes you'd have done the same.")

There was no little ambiguity in the fact that many of the actors were playing parts which "Monty" Mackenzie had based, more or less recognisably, on living Barra characters — most of whom were identified locally by patronymics or nicknames. Gordon Jackson asked his landlady, Mrs Haggerty of Brevig, about the local original of his part, the mother-pecked George

Campbell. "Oh," replied Mrs Haggerty, "you're The Dirt." Jackson inquired no further. Monja Danischewsky, who lodged with the Castlebay headmaster, Neil Angus Macdonald, partly because his was one of the few houses with a bathroom, was introduced early on to Father John Macmillan (Fr James MacAlister in Mackenzie's books) at the small house to which this renowned priest had retired, to write Greek verse, tell Gaelic stories, read stories of the Wild West, wait eagerly for the football results, and celebrate Mass in the shed by his house which, because of his debilitating illness, had been consecrated as a chapel.

Danischewsky was taken early to see Fr Macmillan, as part of Compton Mackenzie's plan to "ingratiate" the film people with the locals. It was a typically unforgettable meeting. The fledgling producer lowered himself nervously into a chair in the priest's living-room, and Fr John promptly rose to his full, impressive height and took a step towards Danischewsky with a forbidding frown on his face. "Look out!" he boomed, "You are sitting on the Pope!" Danischewsky jumped from the chair. He had sat down on the breviary.

Later they went to see the celebrated chapel in the shed:

We went through the kitchen, neat and comfortable, and presided over by his devoted housekeeper, Matilda MacPhee, and then out of the back door past a dustbin. A sheep and a black and white lamb scattered away from us as we went over to a couple of small sheds. One of these he referred to as the "dry necessary", the other shed, hardly bigger, was the chapel, with the same white painted little window, but on this one a rough cross had been scratched in the paint. The altar was made of a table covered with an embroidered cloth, and set with two jars of artificial flowers under a picture of the

Madonna, hung against the cloth on the wall. There was a silver chalice, engraved in the Gaelic, which had been presented to Fr John on the occasion of his celebrating the first Mass on St Kilda after many, many years. He rubbed this affectionately with his fingers as he showed it to me; it had no time to get tarnished. There was a dusty memorial card on the wall, for the son The Coddy had lost in the war . . .

Danischewsky, whose idea of a servant of the Gospel was a confusion of Church of England vicars, oligarchs of the Orthodoxy, and, perhaps, Scottish sabbatarians, anxiously checked with Father John Macmillan if it would be within the remit of the faith of the people of the southern isles to allow the taking of whisky from a foundered ship on Sundays. The priest looked surprised. "And what better day," he said, "for stealing the whisky, than the Lord's own day?"

Fr Macmillan died shortly afterwards. On a final visit Danischewsky took him a bottle of whisky. Before opening it, the Russian ritually turned it upside down. Catching the priest's look askance, he asked if that was not a proper procedure.

"Am I wrong to do it, Father? I was told it's a good idea."

"Aye," said Father Macmillan, smiling, "it's a good idea right enough, if you have the time."

If Father Macmillan approved of his people relieving the stricken ship of her cargo, Danischewsky was soon to discover, to his surprise and dismay, that his director, Sandy Mackendrick, did not. Mackendrick had been reared in Glasgow by a strictly Calvinist grandmother before becoming a graphic designer, working for a wartime film unit in Italy, and finally returning to civilian life at Ealing, where he gained a deserved reputation for meticulously working out "set-ups" – breaking down scripts into minute detail, and illustrating intricate individual scenes which would then be transferred to camera-shots. *Whisky Galore!* being his first film, the Scot was obsessively concerned with every aspect of its making, which led to endless friction with his producer. "It turned out," recalled Danischewsky, "to be a miserable if successful collaboration."

The strained atmosphere was not helped by Mackendrick's growing conviction that the islanders had been quite at fault. While Danischewsky – in common, to be fair, with most of the cast, with Compton Mackenzie, and with several hundred thousand readers of the book – saw the people of the islands as the charming, feckless heroes of the tale, Alexander Mackendrick increasingly took the part of Captain Paul Waggett, the pompous English landowner who Mackenzie had based on Barra's unsuspecting doctor, and who spends most of the story in a state of futile spluttering incomprehension of the islanders' inability to play the game by the book. Mackendrick simply thought that Waggett had been right and the islanders wrong. He would brook no debate on the subject, once turning on Danischewsky and angrily accusing him of attempting to turn the film into a "Jewish folk comedy". That other Presbyterian Scot, Charles McColl, would have relished Sandy Mackendrick's support. But they were both too late for that, and the only result of the director's unpopular stance was to elevate Basil Radford's portrayal of Waggett out of the realms of clownish caricature and to invest the captain of the Home Guard with a degree of sympathy which Mackenzie, certainly, had never intended.

So filming progressed throughout that wet summer in Barra, with no more and no less friction and agreement, laughter and dismay than was considered usual for such ventures, despite the fact that the small island was playing host to the largest location film unit ever to leave a British studio. The people of Northbay saw their church hall fitted out as an indoor studio. The Castlebay hall was turned into a small projection theatre for the film's rushes, and doubled up as a cinema where some recent films were shown – largely to the disinterest of the islanders. A cowshed became the canteen, a byre the carpentry shop, a generator was shipped to the electricity-free island to power the lights and cameras. Aeroplanes of the British European Airlines flew in and out of the Traigh Mhor with reels of film, major and minor actors and actresses, boxes of make-up and crates of machine-parts.

Here and there the islanders would catch a glimpse of an oddly memorable sight, such as Chrissie MacSween, Compton Mackenzie's secretary (and, later, his second wife), whose family was from the small island of Scalpay, off Harris, coaching Joan Greenwood into an admirable island accent, or Mackenzie himself, crippled as so often by sciatica, limping from set to set with the inflated inner-tube of a car tyre under his arm – "Compton's bum-ring". But largely they had jobs to go to and a life of their own to lead, and they did so unperturbed by the fame and affluence which surrounded them – even if, at the end of the day, they retired to a makeshift bed in the living-room, their own having been rented to a clapper-board man. When there was a contact between the two groups, it was usually the "fillums" who found themselves impressed. Monja Danischewsky was in a local house one day when its owner returned home from working on upgrading the island's only road.

"I believe you're Russian?" he inquired of Danischewsky. The producer said that he was.

"Then I'm wondering," the man went on, "if you can tell me why jealousy is such a recurring theme with Tolstoy's heroines?"

Rationing was still in force throughout Britain in 1948, and although the film unit put a strain on some local resources – such as the water supply, and the few cars and lorries – the influx of hard cash and of a supply of tinned and dried foodstuffs was welcomed.

But there was one rather large irony. With the cargo of the *Politician* mostly exhausted (although a bottle or two remained, and was politely doled out to the distinguished visitors), Barra was short of whisky. For the purposes of filming, Ealing Studios had to send to the southern isles three dozen dummy bottles of Scotch, made of wax.

By September, when filming was completed, to his chagrin Danischewsky had run over budget by £20,000, and a couple of scenes had still to be shot back in the comfort of Ealing Studios. It had been a hectic and often harrowing experience for both producer and director, and neither was confident of the film's success. Danischewsky was gloomily convinced that the story had a monosexual appeal, fine for men, but unattractive to the female audience which was so necessary at the box-office. "How the hell," he asked at the final studio showing, "are we going to get the women in to see it?" Sandy Mackendrick, having packed away the final reel, turned to Gordon Jackson and said, confidentially, that *Whisky Galore!* would "probably turn out to be a dull documentary on island life".

Whisky Galore! was not, in fact, riotously acclaimed by the critics following its West End launch at the Haymarket Gaumont on 16 June 1949. This was a glorious age for Ealing Studios, and Mackendrick's modest Scottish comedy suffered, at the time, under the shadow of *Passport to Pimlico* (which was breaking box-office records) and *Kind Hearts and Coronets* (which was released in the same week). The *Sunday Times* judged that "it will do", despite lacking "the richness of comic invention of *Passport to Pimlico*". The *Daily Herald* found it "sunny, friendly and gay . . . [although it] jabbers and havers and sprawls all over the place like a leggy new-born colt".

Whisky Galore! may have been a slow starter, but it turned out to have staying power – rarely has a day passed since 1949 without it being shown, on a cinema or a television screen, somewhere in the world. For its other great, and quite unanticipated, merit has proven to be its international appeal.

Whisky Galore! was seen from the beginning as a quintessentially British comedy. Although the book had sold well in the United States, it was thought that the combination of Scottish accents, British character actors and the mildly morbid fatalism of Mackendrick's direction would make the film quite inaccessible to foreign audiences. Even the title was untranslatable (*Whisky Galore* is probably the only best-selling book and certainly the only major film to have taken its name entirely from Scottish Gaelic: *uisge beatha* being whisky, and *gu leoir* meaning plenteous).

The studio bosses were right on the last point. They actually had tried to alter the name before the film's British release, preferring *Golden Treasure* or *Liquid Treasure,* but were convinced by Compton Mackenzie that in a period of austerity the words *Whisky Galore!* outside a cinema would prove to be an irresistible draw. The Americans would, however, have none of it, and opted for *Tight Little Island,* which was not bad, although some years later Monja Danichewsky bumped into the veteran American humorist James Thurber who told him: "I wish I'd known you at the time; the right American title for the film is 'Scotch on the Rocks'."

The French, free from the tasteful restraints of Ealing Studios dubbed the film *Whisky-a-go-go.* It opened at the Cinema Marbeuf in Paris in September 1950 and attracted 20,000 paying customers in its first five days. "Nothing but praise," the cinema's manager, M. Marsac, was moved to write to Eagle-Lion Distributors in London, "nothing but praise is heard from the crowds leaving the hall. We shall do wonderful business together with this picture, which is breaking all records in this cinema." Compton Mackenzie was flown out to Paris and feted by cinemaphile and literati alike. "The humour," one Frenchman told him in wonderment, "in *Whisky-a-go-go* is a surprise to us. For an Englishman, it is so *Gallic.*" If the use of "galore" as an adverbal or adjectival suffix entered the popular vocabulary as a result of the film in Britain, so also *Whisky-a-go-go* had a lasting impact in France: it was adopted as the name of bars and nightclubs throughout the country.

And, of course, the whisky industry benefited. Danischewsky estimated that, in America, "the film sold more Scotch than the advertisements". Michael Balcon admitted that he was "convinced that our film helped to bring about a change in the drinking habits in France, which has become a whisky-drinking country to an extent no one could have believed possible. Trade follows the film!"

The industry recognised its debt on at least one grand occasion. When the film had become a demonstrable international success the Distillers Company Ltd threw a party at the Savoy Hotel for everyone concerned. An epicurean dinner, Michael Balcon recalled, was accompanied by wines and liqueurs, and finally each guest was presented, at the table, with a full bottle of whisky on the proviso that he drink it before leaving. Each man did, Balcon records. "There were no breathalyser tests then!"

There were no crusading Customs and Excise officers in the book or the film of *Whisky Galore!* No pensioners were threatened by severe legal action and nobody was sent to jail. In his inspired flight of fancy Mackenzie took a rough and sober canvas and painted brilliantly upon it with primary colours.

But the deep regard for the people of the Hebrides which informed all of Mackenzie's Highland fictions, which insured them from patronage or mockery and which elevated them beyond any similar efforts written before or since, also surfaced when he came to talk of the realities of the affair of the SS *Politician*. Like many people he thought that the islanders' biggest mistake was to sell whisky to the labourers at the Balivanich aerodrome building sites.

> That of course was a very foolish thing to do, selling it to those people making the Benbecula aerodrome. And of course that was the temptation, because they had the money, that was the temptation . . .
>
> But the people had a perfect right. They were rescuing it, they weren't looting it at all. The law doesn't come into it. It's gift from Almighty God to them, there it comes, it's been a tradition for centuries and centuries that in Cornwall, Wales and the west, what the sea gives is a gift. Of course in the days when they deliberately had false lights, then it becomes a crime, but what comes from the sea should go to the people. I feel this very strongly . . . It's no good talking about looting or anything like that.

Whisky Galore was Compton Mackenzie's legacy to the southern isles, and unlike many another literary offering it was welcomed by the legatees. The story which he loosely based on some occasionally grim incidents is free from malice and condescension. Unlike other comic writers on the Highlands and Islands Mackenzie attempted no cheap laughs at the expense of the native people. Even the hiccups of Hebridean English, winningly dissembled by an author who had taken the trouble to learn some Gaelic, seem to reflect more disparagingly upon Mackenzie's native tongue than upon Gaelic. The figure most keenly lampooned, the luckless Captain Paul Waggett, actually shared much with Mackenzie himself – they were both transplanted Englishmen (Mackenzie was born in County Durham), both had the sporting rights of part of the islands, and both were captains of the Home Guard. The true story of the *Politician,* as celebrated by the people of the southern isles in song, story and drama, has clearly become a part of folklore. The story of the SS *Cabinet Minister* and the two Toddays, the story of Sergeant Odd and his Peigi, of George Campbell and his draconian mother, of Father James MacAlister and Duncan Macroon, survives for different reasons. In it Mackenzie embroidered a world which, like the one created by his friend and admirer P.G. Wodehouse, is only recognisable in our dreams. Its characters flit easily along the sunlit edges of reality, enchanting, untouchable and innocent of any mundane misdeed. Their lives and their aspirations are uncomplicated, easy to grasp and even easier to wish upon oneself.

Of all the places across the world in which he lingered, Compton Mackenzie considered that in the southern isles of the Outer Hebrides that mirage came closest to reality. It is why he was buried there in 1972, among his friends, beneath a modest cross in the marram grass, where once he saw the flotsam from torpedoed ships wash up on to the shore and where the clear blue sea of the Hebrides frames, as it always has, the everyday life of ordinary people.

Postscript

From The Times, London, 20 January 1990
"A TOT OF WHISKY GALORE UNDER THE FLOOR"

A cache of whisky removed from the wreck of the SS *Politician,* which sank off the Isle of Eriskay nearly 50 years ago, prompting Sir Compton Mackenzie's novel *Whisky Galore,* has been discovered under the floor of a croft on the neighbouring island of Barra.

The four bottles were only found during repairs by the owner, Mr David Barston, when a floorboard suddenly popped up near the spot where he was working, disclosing the bottles of White Horse whisky.

"It was a very skilled piece of joinery. You would not have known it was there," said Mr Barston, a former Lancashire blacksmith and furniture-maker. "There were two full-sized bottles lying flat and two half-bottles standing up in the corner at the back. However, some of the whisky had evaporated because the seals on the corks had worn away."

The bottles may well have been hidden in 1941 and forgotten as the years passed.

Whisky from the wreck changes hands for considerable sums of money. Two years ago, eight bottles from the ship, which foundered in a gale in the Sound of Eriskay in 1941, fetched

£4,000 when auctioned at Christie's. Mr Barston, however, said he was not interested in selling. The bottles, he said, belonged to the island.

"I will probably put one into the local museum, and perhaps another at the airport, where I work as a part-time fireman. I will keep the others," he said.

The croft has been empty for the past four years. Before that, it belonged to the Macdonald family, in which there were three brothers who were fishermen.

A spokesman for White Horse said they would be interested in acquiring one of the bottles.

Bibliography

Goodrich-Freer's harrowing account of her visit to the Uists at the turn of the century, quoted in Chapter Two, is from her book *Outer Isles* (1901). The rather more cheerful stories of life in Barra during the first half of this century are taken largely from *A View of Barra* by Donald Buchanan (1941). Two autobiographies, *Michael Balcon Presents . . .* and *White Russian – Red Face,* by Monja Danischewsky, helped me piece together the story of the making of the film (they are remarkably unanimous). Compton Mackenzie's *My Life and Times,* Octaves Seven, Eight and Nine were essential reading; Alastair Alpin MacGregor's *The Western Isles* was not essential reading but is now, as it was when published, good for a laugh. *Benbecula* by Ray Burnett is a fascinating history of the dark island and was particularly useful in its coverage of the 1920s and 1930s land raids. *The Scots Magazine* was an excellent source of unusual material.

I am very grateful to Margaret Fay Shaw for allowing me to borrow, from her *Folksongs and Folklore of South Uist,* the quotes at the head of Chapters One, Two and Seven, and her transcription of Roderick Campbell's *Oran na Politician* in Chapter Eight. John Lorne Campbell equally kindly permitted me to use, in Chapter Four, Ronald's story, from his *Tales from Barra as Told by the Coddy.* The Sea Blessing at the head of Chapter Three is taken – not, sadly, in its entirety – from Carmichael's *Carmina Gadelica*.

The book which started it all, Compton Mackenzie's *Whisky Galore,* has sold countless millions of copies around the world and is presently in its tenth Penguin imprint. It seems to need no recommendation from me.

Index

Abelia 38

Admiral 8, 9

The Antiquary whisky on board '*Polly*' 34

Arandora Star 23

Arnott Young Ltd of Dalmuir 67, 75, 116

Assistance (salvage steamer) 67–8, 75, 100, 108, 115

Attendant (salvage vessel) 110

Balcon, Sir Michael 137, 145

Ballantine's whisky on board '*Polly*' 34

Bank of England 116

Barra ix, 3, 5, 6, 79, 104, 143, 149–50

    Barra Company, Home Guard 22–3

    Barra lifeboat 41

    Ealing Studios film crew, arrival on 137–8

    filming of *Whisky Galore!* on 141–3

    Local Defence Volunteers (LDV) on 134–5

    rationing in force on 142–3

Barston, David 149–50

Bartlett, Dr Samuel (Barra) 22–3

Bell, Mike (finance broker) 124, 126

Benbecula 3, 4, 24, 58, 59, 66, 80–81, 98–9, 107, 114, 146

SS *Birchol*, wrecked on South Uist (1940) 38

Blue Funnel Line 5

Board of Agriculture in Scotland (BOAS) 15

Bootham White, Edward (Tarbert customs officer) 85–7

St Brendan 48

British Film Institute xii

British Iron and Steel Corporation (Salvage) Ltd 66–7, 75, 109

Brough, Jeremy 124–5, 126

Buchanan, Dr Donald of Barra 5

Buchanan, Michael (radical spokesman on Barra) 10–11

Buncher, Captain (character in *Whisky Galore*) 137

Bunmhullin on Eriskay 1

SS *Cabinet Minister* (fictional '*Polly*') 133–4, 147

Calvay Island 36, 77

Campbell, George (character in *Whisky Galore*) 138–9, 147

Campbell, James 72, 82, 89, 94

Campbell, John Lorne 51

Campbell, Neil 72–5, 82, 89, 94

Campbell, Neil (businessman from Skye) 124, 126

Campbell, Roderick 89

    Oran na Politician (*Song of the*

Politician commemorating
events) 128–32
Campbell of Lochboisdale, Angus
John 49, 89, 94, 112, 128
Capaldi (diver and café owner from
Lewis) 120, 121
Carnival (Mackenzie, C.) 134
Caroline Moller (salvage vessel)
108–9
Castlebay on Barra 78, 137, 138,
141–2
Cathcart, Lady Gordon (daughter of
John Gordon) 10–11, 14–15,
16, 24–5
Charente Steamship Company 29
Christie's (auctioneers) 124, 125,
149–50
Churchill Baron Financial Services
124–5
Colonial Office, security Branch of
117–18
Commissioners of Customs &
Excise, London 62, 75–6,
97–8, 99–102
Cotteen (coaster on salvage duty for
SS *Politician*) 43
Creagorry Hotel 24, 59, 93
Crofter's Commission 12
Crofting Act (1886) 11
Cumbrae Head 76
HM Customs & Excise xii, 33, 53,
59, 60, 61, 69–72, 77, 113,
121
  clearing Hold Five, Gledhill's
  report on 75–6
  Collector in Inverness, plea for
  destruction of dutiable goods
  to 110–11
  complaints on police omissions
  (and response of Chief
  Constable to) 97–8, 99–102
  crusading officers in *Whisky
  Galore*, lack of 145

Customs Consolidation Act
(1876) 97, 102
dismissal of theft charges 102–5
disposition on alcoholic cargo left
aboard '*Polly*' 44–5
Gauger (customs officer) 63–4,
70
organisation in Hebrides of 61–2
powers of officers of 82
raids on crofts and houses 86–7, 90
redeemable cargo from Hold
Five, shipping out of 106

Daily Herald 143
Daily Mail 118
HMT *Dalmatia* 74
Danischewsky, Monja 137, 138,
141, 142, 144, 145
Davidson, Ian (Stornoway hotelier)
120–21
De La Rue of London xi, 33, 118
Distillers Company Ltd 145
Donald, D.A., Sheriff-substitute at
Lochmaddy 78, 85, 88, 93
Duggan, Farther Dermit 4–5

Ealing Studios 136–7, 137–8
irony of shortage of whisky on Barra
for 143
Edward VIII xi
Eoligarry on Barra 13–14, 23, 79
Eriskay ix, 1, 3, 53, 104, 134, 149
  draconian crackdown, resentment
  at 53
  Jamaican banknotes, inventive
  uses of 55–6
  'The King's Ransom', Ronald and
  51–3
  lack of toxicity of spirits from
  '*Polly*,' stories about 53–4
  raids on crofts and houses on
  86–7, 90
  small boats, congregation on 48

Eugenia Emberikos, wrecked on east of Barra 23

Flynn, Errol 118–19
Food Production Committee in Lochboisdale 21
The Four Winds of Love quartet (Mackenzie, C.) 134
Fraser, Chief Constable William 85–6, 99–102
Furness, Withy & Co. Ltd 27–9

Gairloch 48
Garrynamonie on South Uist 63, 82–3, 127–8
Gledhill, Ivan (Customs & Excise surveyor in Portree) 61, 66, 90, 110
  condition of '*Polly,*' letter from Holden concerning 67–8
  confiscation of boats 93–7
  dismissal of theft charges 102–5
  explosives on '*Polly,*' request for use of 110–11
  final report from 112–15
  leniency of sentences 90–91
  'looted uncustomed spirits,' complaints about 97–8, 99–102
  police accounts of activities, difference from those of 86–8
  property in wrecks, musing on islanders' attitude to 81
  prosecution of Barra men 79, 80–81
  raids, spectacular lack of success of 86
  refloating of '*Polly,*' witness to 108
  reinforcements, call for 85–6
  seal on Hold Five, attachment of 64–5
  unloading whisky, priority given to 75–6
  vandalism in Lochboisdale, concerns about 91–2
  wrathful campaign against 'looters', 69, 85–6
Glendale Bay 83
Goodrich-Freer, Ada 12
Gray, John, Lochmaddy public prosecutor 81, 85, 89, 90–91, 93, 102, 128
Great Todday (Todaidh Mór, 'Barra' in *Whisky Galore*) 135, 147
Greenshields, Cowie & Co. Ltd, Crown Agents 33
Greenwood, Joan 137, 138, 142
Gulf Stream 3

Haig & Haig's whisky on board '*Polly*' 34
Harris, small boats congregation on Eriskay from 48
Harrison Lines of Liverpool 28, 42–3, 44, 45, 47, 109
Haun anchorage on Eriskay 96
Highland News 92
Holden, Percy (Arnott Young site agent in Lochboisdale) 67–8, 76, 106, 108, 111–12, 120
Hore Belisha, Leslie (War Minister) 18–19
Hunting the Fairies (Mackenzie, C.) 136

Iacain, Alastair 55
Inverness Prison 89, 91, 92, 127

Jackson, Gordon 137, 138–9, 143
Jamaica Queen washed up at Eoligarry, Barra 23
Jamaican currency notes x–xi, 33, 55–6, 116–18, 125

James Buchanan's whisky on board '*Polly*' 34

James Martin's whisky on board '*Polly*' 34

J.B. Cousins (marine survey company) 109

John Brown of Clydebank 27 10,

John Gordon of Cluny Castle, 7–9

John of Boisdale, Angus 55

Johnnie Walker Red and Black Label whisky on board '*Polly*' 34

Johnston, Tom, Secretary of State for Scotland 33, 56–7, 107

St Joseph (flat-bottomed motorised boat) 62, 63–4, 69, 71, 82, 83

Kay, Commander (chief salvage officer) 62, 65–6, 75, 109, 112–13

salvage operation on '*Polly*' 42–4, 47

Keep the Home Guard Turning (Mackenzie, C.) 134–5, 136

King George IV whisky on board '*Polly*' 34

King William IV whisky on board '*Polly*' 34

King's Pipe (furnace for customs' confiscated goods) 110–11

King's Ransom whisky on board '*Polly*' 34

Kyle of Lochalsh 48

Laing, Reverend Malcolm 85, 88

Lasser, Lieutenant Georg (U-boat commander) 45

Lauretson, Captain Edward 67, 68, 75–6, 106, 108, 110

Lewis 48

Little Todday (Todaidh Beag, 'Vatersay' in *Whisky Galore*) 135, 147

Liverpool and Glasgow Salvage Association 42–3, 44

Lloyds of London 117

Lloyd's Registry 38

Local Government Board 13–14

Loch Boisdale 70–71, 107

Lochboisdale 8, 17, 22, 42, 49–50, 71–2, 81, 113, 115

Customs & Excise base at 60

Food Production Committee in 21

Neil Campbell's landing at 74–5

police station at 64–5, 100

salvage work from, memories of 76–7

vandalism in, prison sentences and 91–2

whisky from '*Polly*,' 'salvage' to Lochboisdale of 71–2

Lochboisdale Hotel 57, 64

Lochmaddy 5

Procurator-Fiscal at 65, 81, 84, 85, 90, 98, 102, 128

Sheriff Court at 78–80, 85, 88–91, 92–3, 107

SS *London Commerce* (later SS *Collegian*) 27–8

SS *London Importer* (later SS *Reliant*) 27–8

SS *London Mariner* (later SS *Craftsman*) 27–8

SS *London Merchant* (later SS *Politician*) 27–8

SS *London Shipper* (later SS *Statesman*) 27–8

Ludag on South Uist 54, 55, 62, 63–4, 83

MacAulay, Donald (publican at Balivanich) 24–5, 59

MacAulay, Jessie 127

MacCormack, Kenny (Sir Compton's driver on Barra) 133–4

MacDiarmid of Ardnamurchan, Donald 76–7

MacDonald, John, Cathcart factor in South Uist 15–16, 24–5

Macdonald, Neil Angus (Castlebay headmaster) 139

Macdonald, Ramsay 15

MacGregor, Alastair Alpin 132–3, 135

MacInnes, Duncan 49–50, 55
  memories of finding grounded '*Polly*' 39–40
  stealing of goods from '*Polly*', problem of 53
  witness to looting by naval trawler crew 58

MacInnes, John, local government officer for Benbecula, South Uist and Eriskay 84, 85, 88

Macintosh, Charles Fraser 10

Mackendrick, Alexander 137, 140–41, 143

Mackenzie, Captain Finlay 21–2, 22–35 7–8, 64

Mackenzie, Constable Donald 62, 63, 64–5, 69, 72, 79, 82, 86, 88
  haul from '*Polly*' by Uistmen, capture of 70–71
  whisky from '*Polly*' entrusted to care of 115

Mackenzie, Sir Compton 18, 21–2 51, 56–7, 58–9, 119, 127, 134, 142, 145, 147

Maclean, Cailean xii

Maclean, Dr Alasdair xii

Macmillan, Father John 135, 139–40

MacMillan, Malcolm K. 17

Macmillan, Procurator Fiscal Donald 102–4

MacMillan of Kilphedar, Norman 48–9, 54

MacNeil, Coxwain Murdo (Castlebay lifeboat) 41

MacNeil, William Og of Bruernish 13–14

MacPhee, Angus (radical spokesman on Benbecula) 11

MacPhee, Donald (professional diver) 122–4, 126

MacPhee, Matilda (housekeeper for Father MacMillan) 139

MacPherson, John the 'Coddy' of Barra 50–51, 56, 135, 138, 140, 151–2

MacSween, Chrissie (later Lady Mackenzie) 142

Mail on Sunday 123

Mallaig 48

SS *Manchester Regiment* 27–8

Marauder (salvage boat) 108

Marconi International Marine Communications Company 42

Matheson, Sir William 9

McCallum's Perfection whisky on board '*Polly*' 34

McColl, Charles (Customs & Excise) 81, 86, 87–8, 94, 96, 110, 141
  character and background 60–65
  condition of '*Polly*', despair about 67–8
  confiscation of boats 93–6
  Customs & Excise Act, punitive use 65, 80–81, 90
  dismissal of theft charges 102–5
  dissatisfaction with salvage operation 65–6
  dutiable cargo remaining on '*Polly*', demolition of (August 1942) 111–12
  final report from (Autumn 1942) 112–15

and Hold Five 64–5, 77–8

legal authorities, pressure for stiff
    sentences put on 90

leniency of sentences, protests
    about 90–91

local citizenry, suspicions of 62–3

looted uncustomed spirits,
    complaint about police on
    97–8, 99–102

mission against sailing boats, *St
    Joseph* and 62–4, 70–72, 83–4,
    94, 95–6

police accounts of activities,
    difference from those of 86–8

powers of customs officials,
    exercise of 82

prosecution of Barra men 79,
    80–81

rampant vandalism on
    '*Polly*'assertions of 68–9

refloating of '*Polly*', witness to
    108

resale of confiscated vessels to
    owners, authorisation for 104

robbery from Revenue, belief in
    enormous scale of 65–6

unloading whisky, priority given
    to 75, 76

vandalism against, blaming
    'looters' for 91–2

McColl, Father Donald 10–11

McDonald, Allan xii

McDougall, Roderick of Kentangval
    5

McNeil, Jonathan, of Glen
    Castlebay 5

McNeil of Garynamonie, Donald
    Hector 54–5 63–4, 82–3, 89

Merchant Ship Act (1894) 46

Minch 4, 21, 34, 35, 36, 42, 46–7,
    57, 108

Mitchell, Air Chief Marshal Sir
    William 56

Moidart 3–4

The Monarch of the Glen
    (Mackenzie, C.) 134, 135

Mossman, Chief Engineer on SS
    Politician 37, 45

Mountain Dew whisky on board
    '*Polly*' 34

Mull 48

Napier Commission (1883) 8, 10,
    11

Nassau, Bahamas xi

National Records Offices,
    Edinburgh and London xii

National Union of Seamen xii

North Boisdale on South Uist 64

North Uist 3, 4–5, 6–7, 17, 79,
    92–3

Northbay on Barra 79, 137, 141

Oak Crest, torpedoed in North
    Atlantic 23

Oban 48

Old Curio whisky on board '*Polly*'
    34

Passport to Pimlico (film directed by
    Henry Cornelius) 143

St Patrick 48

PD Special whisky on board '*Polly*'
    34

Peter Mackenzie's whisky on board
    '*Polly*' 34

SS *Politician* ix, 34, 35, 62, 66, 78,
    99, 100, 103, 105–6

    Admiralty service in Second
        World War 29–30

    afterlife of 119

    anniversary dive on wreck of (and
        findings from) 120–21

    Battle of the Atlantic for 30–32

    Crown seals on, coasting crews
        scant respect for 107

Customs & Excise on alcoholic
cargo left aboard 44–5
damage after re-float mishap
108–9
distress signals from 38
dubbed '*Polly*' by islanders 47
duty on bottles missing from,
write-off of 107–8
duty-free nature of whisky on
board 34
early contacts of islanders with
wreck of (and boarding by)
47–8
evacuation of crew from 41–2
grounding on Eriskay
36–769–70,
Highland News headline story on
92–3
insurance value of 42
Jamaican currency stored in Hold
Five 33
joint operation to reclaim lost
cargo from 87–8
Lifeboat Four, launch of 39
mysterious incident following
affair of 115–16
oil in hold of 55–6
post-grounding action aboard
39
recreational diving on wreck of
120, 121–2
re-floating of (September 1941)
108
relaunch of, rejection of idea for
109
salvage authorities final plan for
109–10
salvage of 43–4
salvage operation, 1990 plan for
126
salvage potential of superstructure
of 66–7
salvaged whisky from 107

salvaging of steel from 112
scuttling of 108–9
tales of Eriskay and grounding of
50–59
undamaged cargo, removal of 44
vessels spotted leaving, pursuit of
83–4
whisky bottles in Hold Five
33–4
SS Politician plc. 124–6
Pollachar on South Uist 64, 118

Quebec Times (1851) 8

Radford, Basil 137, 138, 141
SS *Ranger* (salvage steamer) 43, 44,
47, 65
Raymond, Harold (Chatto &
Windus) 135–6
Richards, Sergeant G.N. 86–7
Rosinish Point on Eriskay 1, 36,
39
Royal Navy 5, 23
Ru Melvich on Eriskay 36, 38, 123
Rubha Dubh, cliff-face of 40, 41,
47

Samuel Dexter, wrecked in Sound of
Barra 23
Scalpay, Isle of 142
Sea Act, Section 206 of (1876) 101
Second World War xii, 17–25,
119–20
Seton, Bruce 137
Shaw, Margaret Fay 128–32
Shipping and Seamen, General
Register and Record of xii
Sinister Street (Mackenzie, C.) 134
Skye 3–4, 48
Song of the Politician
(commemorating events on)
128–32
Sound of Barra x, 23, 41

Sound of Eriskay ix, 25, 37, 41, 76–7, 88, 96, 108, 115, 109, 120–21

South Glendale on South Uist 1, 25, 107

South Uist 1, 3, 5, 9, 86–7, 90 93–7 104, 113, 122

Spey Royal whisky on board '*Polly*' 34

Stephens, Sergeant Arnold 86–7

Summary Jurisdiction Act (1908) 80–81

Sunday Dispatch 116, 118

Sunday Times 143

Supply Ministry 67, 75

Swain, R.S., Mate on *SS Politician* 35, 37–8, 41, 45

Tales from Barra as Told by Coddy (Campbell, J.L.) 151–2

SS *Thala*, 38, 42, 67, 68

Thos. and Jas. Harrison Ltd, Liverpool xii

Traigh Mhor in Barra 17–18, 21–2, 56–7, 107, 134, 138, 142

HM Treasury 65

Valentine, Reg (international diver) 120–21

Vatersay 3, 8, 14, 20, 40–41, 79

Victoria Vat whisky on board '*Polly*' 34

VVO Gold Bar whisky on board '*Polly*' 34

Waggett, Captain Paul (character in *Keep the Home Guard Turning*) 22–3, 135, 141, 146–7

Whisky Galore (novel by Mackenzie, C.) xii, 120, 149, 152
epic success of 136
legend of 124
Mackenzie's personal reflections on affair of SS *Politician* 145–7
writing and publication of 135–7

Whisky Galore! (film by Alexander Mackendrick) 136–45
premiere of 143
naming of, controversy about 144

White Horse whisky 34, 149–50

William Gilbey Ltd 83

Windsor, Duke and Duchess of xi, 118

Worthington, Captain Beaconsfield *(SS Politician)* 32–3, 34–5, 37, 39, 41, 38, 45, 47, 104–5, 137
cleared of all blame 45
misfortunes of (November 1942) 45

Zembra, Island of 120